MILLARD
FILLMORE

✓ Y0-BZH-153

Rachelle Moyer Francis

Enslow Publishers, Inc.

40 Industrial Road   PO Box 38
Box 398   Aldershot
Berkeley Heights, NJ 07922   Hants GU12 6BP
USA   UK

http://www.enslow.com

Dedication

To Dorothy M. Francis, who started me on this path.

Acknowledgments

Millard and I have had a long path together since 1979 when my mother-in-law, Dorothy Francis, thought my training and energies would be useful at the brand new Millard Fillmore Museum. When I learned his story and wondered why everybody did not know of his inspirational life, Dorothy inspired me to be the one to write it.

In 1987 my husband Doug bought me my first computer and we were off on research. As an at-home mom in those days, I took my children to travel all over New York State and to Washington, D.C. to see first-hand Millard's significant sites. Thank you, Jake, Adam, Bethany and Sara, for being willing to be more "museumed" than most children!

Bill Scheider and Rick Ohler provided very helpful insights and assistance as readers of my text. My class at Eggert listened to every chapter and told me what was boring and what they liked (actually they were so kind and said they liked it all!)

Thanks to Enslow Publishing for making this version possible and to Mary Hull for her brilliant editing. Without Dr. Joseph Bieron and his belief in this project, Millard would still be on the back burner somewhere. Mary Lu Littlefield gave the text its special look and worked with my quilt portrait of Millard so that it could be on the cover. Thanks most especially to Diane Meade and the Aurora Historical Society for publishing this book and for supporting any and all study of our favorite son, Millard Fillmore.

Editorial Direction: *Mary E. Hull, Chestnut Productions*

Design: *Lisa Hochstein, Mary Lu Littlefield*

Copyright © 2006 by Enslow Publishers, Inc.

Library of Congress Cataloging-in-Publication Data
ISBN: 1932583-30-0

To Our Readers: We have done our best to make sure all Internet Addresses in this book were active and appropriate when we went to press. However, the author and the publisher have no control over and assume no liability for the material available on those Internet sites or on other Web sites they may link to. Any comments or suggestions can be sent by e-mail to comments@enslow.com or to the address on the back cover.

Illustration Credits: Aurora Historical Society, 10, 42, 88, 112; Buffalo and Erie County Historical Society, 25, 32, 58, 65, 106; Collection of Rachel Francis, 44, 105; Library of Congress, 4, 12, 50, 72, 76, 91.

Source Document Credits: Aurora Historical Society, 48, 110; Buffalo and Erie County Historical Society, 18, 37, 60, 93, 101; Buffalo and Erie County Public Library, 97; Library of Congress, 7, 21, 78, 81, 99.

Cover: Millard Fillmore Patchwork Wall Hanging, designed and worked by the author.

CONTENTS

As vice president, Millard Fillmore brought a return to order in the emotionally-charged atmosphere of the United States Senate, where he presided.

CHAPTER ONE

A NATION
IN TURMOIL

I n an amazing rise from poverty to power, Millard
Fillmore, the new vice president of the United States,
now sat presiding over the Senate in the plush velvets
and gilded woods of the Senate chambers. Just forty-
eight years before, he'd been born in a humble log cabin
in the hills of New York's Finger Lakes. He would never
have guessed he would one day rise to such a high
political office.

But despite this exalted office, Fillmore felt left out
and frustrated. His president, Zachary Taylor, had no
relationship with him—Taylor barely spoke to him and
did not invite him to cabinet meetings.

When the election in November 1848 named the
Whigs, a political party associated chiefly with manufac-
turing, commercial, and financial interests, the winning
party, Fillmore had not yet even met Taylor, his intended

partner for the next four years. Fillmore wrote Taylor a letter with several of his ideas for their administration, including eliminating the national debt and promoting "the great interest of agriculture and commerce by improving rivers and harbors."[1]

The wise letter of advice, based on the experience of Fillmore's four terms in Congress as a New York representative, must have worried Taylor. Or maybe Taylor thought his political inexperience (he had never even voted in an election before becoming president of the United States) would make him vulnerable to being dominated by Fillmore. Taylor had come to the office of the president as a war hero. The Whig party had chosen him as their candidate primarily because of his success as a general in the Mexican American War.

To make things worse, Fillmore's competitor for political offices in New York State, William Seward, and Fillmore's worst enemy, Whig Party boss Thurlow Weed, had befriended President Taylor and filled his ears with warnings to keep his distance from Fillmore. Weed used his newspaper, the *Albany Evening Journal*, to tear apart the reputation of Fillmore, his former friend and colleague.[2]

Finally Taylor and Fillmore met at the inauguration on Monday, March 5, 1849. Taylor had refused to be inaugurated on Sunday, leaving the country technically without a president for one day. Martial music, a cacophony of bells, whistles, and drums, and the waving of hundreds of flags commemorated the occasion, for this inauguration was attended by more people than ever before. Many of Washington's forty thousand residents and thousands of visitors who came by horse, rail, or water wanted to see

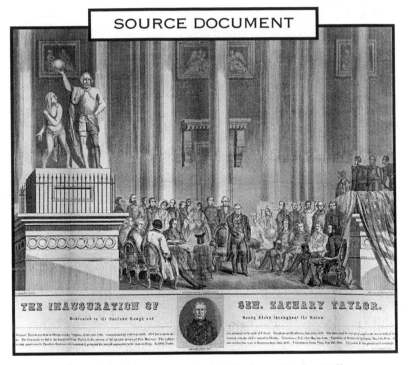

SOURCE DOCUMENT

THE INAUGURATION OF   GEN. ZACHARY TAYLOR.

The March 5, 1849 inauguration of Zachary Taylor. Fillmore was sworn into office as Taylor's vice president on the same day. Though they ran on the Whig ticket together, Taylor was not friendly with Fillmore.

the new president. The diplomats attended in rich and magnificent costumes, the justices of the Supreme Court in their dark robes.

Taylor and Fillmore took their oaths in the Senate chamber. President Taylor delivered his inaugural address from the Eastern Portico of the Capitol and he and Fillmore attended three inaugural balls together until one in the morning.

Not long after this happy occasion however, Fillmore

realized that Taylor's entire cabinet had been poisoned against him. So he devoted all his energy and character to his job of presiding over the Senate. And it needed his attention.

For the last twenty years, vice presidents, whose role was to preside over the Senate, had felt that they had no authority to call senators to order for any violation of courtesy or breaking of the rules. The position had become a largely ceremonial one. By April 3, 1849, Fillmore changed that and announced in a speech that he thought it was his duty to preserve decorum and set rules of order for the Senate. He promised to call any senator to order for any offensive words used. The dignity, courtesy, and calm of Fillmore's tenure in the Senate drew admiration from all sides.

Previously, there had been hostility in the Senate because in 1849 the country was very close to a civil war over the issue of the states' rights to decide the legality of slavery. The nation had been founded under an agreement in the Constitution to ignore the divisive subject of slavery until 1808. The thirteen colonies could never have come together to form a nation if that problem had to be agreed upon beforehand.[3] Now, sixty years later, the practice of slavery had grown so that the South's economy depended on the free labor of slaves. Many in the North deplored slavery. Those who worked to abolish, or end, slavery were known as "abolitionists."

The slavery debate crept into every decision in Congress. For example, there was the question of statehood for California. In 1848, John Sutter had found gold nuggets at his California mill. By the next year, "Forty-niners" from all over the world had flooded into

California to pan for gold and get rich quick. It blossomed from a nearly empty region with scattered ranches and missions to a territory with a population larger and richer than that of some of the original states. The South did not want this big, wealthy region to come into the Union as a free state, weighing with the North. That would upset the precarious political balance of slave versus free in the Senate and House. President Taylor, listening to his abolitionist advisors, Thurlow Weed and William Seward, wanted to let California, Utah, and New Mexico all into the Union as free states, which would have meant instant war with the South.

Seventy three-year-old Senator Henry Clay from Kentucky saw the crisis developing and put his whole intellect and political experience to work to find a way that the conflicting interests could get along and keep the Union together. He thought that the South might let California in as a free state if future states (and not politicians in Washington, D.C.) could decide for themselves whether slavery would be allowed. Letting the voters of a territory decide whether or not slavery would be allowed was a concept known as "popular sovereignty." Henry Clay's Compromise, called the Compromise of 1850, also allowed Utah and New Mexico to organize territorial governments until they had as many people as they needed to become states. As a concession to the North, Clay's Compromise banned slave trading in Washington, D.C., although slavery was still allowed to exist there as long as it existed in Virginia and Maryland as well. Northerners had been sickened at the sight of the slave auctions held right on the Washington Mall, next to the magnificent Smithsonian Castle. The Compromise would eliminate

The United States Senate discusses the Compromise of 1850. At far right, holding the shield of the United States, is Vice President Fillmore, who presided over the Senate at this exciting time. To the left of Fillmore is Daniel Webster. At center stands John C. Calhoun with a quill in his hand, and Henry Clay is seated beside him.

slave auctions in the nation's capitol. The big victory for the South was a more strict enforcement of the fifty-year-old Fugitive Slave Law, which required the return of runaway slaves to their owners.

The Senate debates over the Compromise of 1850 had been getting more heated and wild every day. One spring day in 1850, the hotheaded Senator Henry Foote of Mississippi entered the Senate with a five-chambered pistol, aiming to shoot his opponent, Senator Thomas Hart Benton of Missouri. Fillmore bravely remained in his chair, banging his gavel for order until Foote was restrained and order was restored.[4]

Powerful Senator John C. Calhoun of South Carolina often threatened that the South would secede from, or leave, the Union if things did not go their way. By March of 1850 though, he was so sick, he had his speech read for him in the Senate. Two weeks later, attended by his son, he died in a hotel room. Calhoun was not the only sickened Washington resident. The hot summer breezes from the filthy Potomac River made many ill every summer. Poor sanitation, combined with a swampy location, made the nation's capitol an unhealthy place in the summer, when outbreaks of cholera, typhus, and malaria were common.

As Vice President Fillmore presided over all these debates in the Senate, he remained firm and totally impartial. No one in the Senate knew where Fillmore stood on the Compromise of 1850. But Fillmore thought it would be wise to pay a visit to President Taylor to warn him that if, as presiding officer of the Senate, he were forced to break a tie on Clay's Compromise, he would vote for the measure. "If I should feel it my duty to vote for it, as I might," Fillmore wrote, "I wished him to understand, that it was not out of any hostility to him or his Administration, but the vote would be given, because I deemed it for the interests of the country."[5]

Fillmore was not the only one who felt the Compromise of 1850 was essential to the well-being of the nation. Senator Daniel Webster of Massachusetts swallowed his presidential hopes and endorsed the Compromise after a Senate speech by Henry Clay. A young Illinois lawyer named Abraham Lincoln (who had just left Congress because he was too unpopular to run again for office) also thought the Compromise was

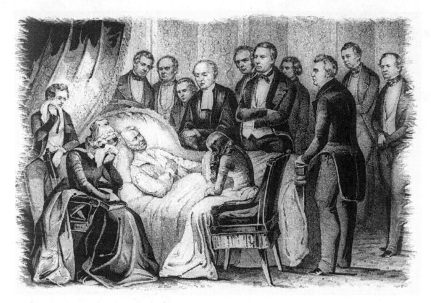

Upon President Taylor's death, Vice President Fillmore was sworn into office and called to lead the country during a time of sectional crisis.

important to keep the country together. But President Taylor was dead against it.[6]

But suddenly and unexpectedly, President Taylor died on July 9, 1850. His doctor had diagnosed him with cholera. At the worst possible time, it became Millard Fillmore's turn to lead the country—with so much agitation and worry, when any decisive move to settle the slavery issue would be greeted by loud and powerful complaints from either the noisy North or the snarling South. The country was in turmoil. Antislavery conventions were being held in the North; secession conventions were raging in the South. California was tired of waiting to become a state. Texas and New Mexico were almost at war over boundary issues. Taylor had brought the country to the brink of civil war in only one-third of a term.

Fillmore was suddenly thrust into the spotlight. He had become president of the United States at a time when the country faced tensions so fierce they threatened to tear it apart. He knew he would have to act wisely yet quickly to avoid trouble.

CHAPTER TWO

THE LOG CABIN

I n the first week of the first year of the nineteenth century, January 7, 1800, Millard Fillmore was born in a humble log cabin, the first white baby to be born in Summer Hill, New York. His mother, Phoebe Millard Fillmore, used a maple sap trough for his cradle.[1]

There was no fancy cradle in the Fillmore's simple home. Their small log cabin had been built about five years before by Millard's father, Nathaniel, while he was still single at age twenty-four. Nathaniel had first ventured alone into the frontier of central New York, traveling on the Great Genesee Road, beyond which there were few settlements.

Land brokers in Vermont had told anyone who would listen about the fertile country of the New York military tract, and he and his brothers were sure that this new land had to be better than their stony Vermont farmland.

Because it experienced financial hardship after the American Revolution, the U.S. government was unable to reward the soldiers of the Revolutionary War and their sons with cash; instead they made land like these hills of the Finger Lakes available at low cost.

So it was that Nathaniel decided to stay in Cayuga County, New York. He cut down the virgin trees, built a rough log cabin, and began to work the land, pulling out and burning stumps and turning up the hard soil to begin a farm.[2] Nathaniel was one of the first to pioneer this densely forested, high, cold ridge. It sat between two long slender Finger Lakes that had been scooped out by the glaciers ten thousand years ago. It was beautiful but completely desolate. The closest neighbors were four miles away. For each human, there were a thousand woodland animals watching silently—wolves, bears, panthers, and deer.

But this was too lonely a life for the sociable and young Nathaniel Fillmore. He had traveled back to Vermont, telling all his family and neighbors of his adventures. In 1797 he married sixteen-year-old Phoebe Millard, the daughter of a doctor, and a year after the birth of their first child Olive, the young family packed up all their meager belongings. Back through the wilderness they traveled, along with Nathaniel's younger brother Calvin and his wife Jerusha. They lived in the log cabin Nathaniel had built in Summer Hill, Cayuga County. It was there that Millard Fillmore was born.

After two summers of backbreaking work, the Fillmore brothers got the discouraging news that they did not have a clear title to this land. The devious land-brokers, peddling these lands to naive farmer-soldiers, often sold the same piece of land to more than one buyer. The true buyer had now shown up to send the disappointed Fillmore families away.

With no more money to buy a new farm, Nathaniel leased a thirteen-acre farm near Sempronius, a few miles north of Millard's birthplace and just a mile west of Skaneateles Lake.[3] It was still forestland, but it was within a fifteen-minute walk of the tiny village of New Hope and a bit of civilization. By now Millard had a baby brother named Cyrus, and it wasn't long before hard-working Nathaniel had his sons helping him clear this new farm and plant crops. He didn't have to worry about losing this farm—it wasn't really his anyway. This was land he would never own, but at least it was a place to live and work to raise food, a little cash, and his growing family.

By the time his next brother, Almon, arrived in 1806, Millard had learned to be a big help with the never-ending labor of pioneering. He could fetch water from the stream that trickled down to the lake. He weeded the vegetable garden, carried wood, and gathered apples from Apple Tree Point.

He liked to work with his dad, but beautiful Skaneateles Lake kept beckoning to him. He knew too well how full of fish it was. He could look deep down into its crystal clear depths and see hundreds right from his canoe. Sometimes it even seemed to Millard that the canoe was suspended in mid-air—it was that clear. He always had to work up his courage, though, to dive into the frigid but refreshing waters of Skaneateles Lake, even in August.

Hunting in the deep woods was always productive,

with wildlife behind every tree. If only young Millard could have a gun. But Nathaniel did not approve of such leisure for his family. He would always say, "No man ever prospered who spent much of his time in hunting and fishing. Those employments are only fit for Indians, or white men no better than Indians."[4]

Perhaps Nathaniel's strong opinions were born out of his great love for the wildlife around him. One day, Millard thoughtlessly killed a mother bird. Nathaniel grieved so much that it made a deep impression on his young son.

> Millard, do you realize what you have done? You have taken the life of a mother, and have left her children to die of starvation in the nest. How would you like to have a great giant come along and kill your father and mother, and leave you alone without food or care?[5]

Nathaniel Fillmore's rebuke sank so deeply into his son's heart that Millard vowed never again to take the life of a living creature.

It was not that Nathaniel was always scolding Millard. Nate loved to read and loved to talk about politics, religion, and farming to his family and any visitor who came along. Before long he was the respected center of his neighborhood.

Finally Millard's parents permitted one diversion from the daily frontier life of hard work. Millard was allowed to go to Mrs. Belcher's school. Nathaniel had actually taught school in 1804 to help Olive and a few others begin to read.[6] But when Mrs. Belcher moved into the area, he was only too happy to hand over the reins of learning to her. She did not have a lot of education herself, but she was only teaching the simplest lessons

SOURCE DOCUMENT

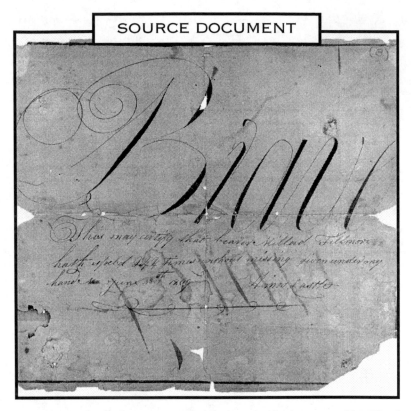

New Hope schoolmaster Amos Castle presented nine-year-old Millard with this "Bravo" award, certifying that "Millard Fillmore hath spel'd 244 times without missing under my hand, June 18, 1809."

of alphabet, spelling, and reading to the small children of New Hope.

On the walk to Mrs. Belcher's school, Millard and his sister Olive always passed Carpenter's Falls. It was not only the best place around Skaneateles Lake to find delicious wild huckleberries, but also a most exciting fifty-foot cascade of rushing water. Some days they would just sit together in the woods, eating those juicy huckleberries and listening to the roar of the waterfall. Carpenter's

Falls was one of Millard's favorite places in his very small world.

School was held in an old deserted log house that had been furnished with a few benches without backs and a board on which to write. Millard loved to go to school, but it never lasted for more than a few months, far too short a time to satisfy his desire to learn. When spring came, it was more important to Millard's father to have help with the farming than for Millard to get a lot of book learning.[7]

So it would be back to the daily work of clearing, plowing, and planting for Millard until the work at the farm let up enough to allow him to return to school for a few more weeks or months. Those ancient glaciers had filled their fields with rocks. Millard had the job of piling every single rock turned up by the plow into a rock wall along the borders of the farm. He expertly used his trusty axe to split firewood for a whole winter's worth of toasty fires. Nathaniel taught his eldest son how to pile the firewood perfectly with neatly criss-crossed stacks at both ends to keep the piles from falling down. Millard also had to split logs to keep the split-rail fences in repair. The corn had to be cut and shucked, grain had to be threshed, hay had to be stacked, and apples picked and dried or pressed into cider.

While he did all his chores, Millard's mind went over and over the latest facts or ideas he had learned in school, until it became so much a part of his understanding that he knew it would never leave him. His seasonal absences from school only made his hunger for learning all the more ravenous.

When Millard was nine, Amos Castle was hired to

conduct school in New Hope and his teaching offered a better education than Millard had yet experienced. This new schoolmaster taught reading, writing, spelling, and arithmetic and he drilled the children thoroughly in Webster's spelling book.

It frustrated Millard, though, that while he could go through Webster's speller and never miss the spelling of a word, he was not taught the definition of a single one of those words. But there was no dictionary in the school, nor had the young scholar ever come across one anywhere else.

The only reading materials in the Fillmore home were a hymnbook, a Bible, and an almanac, with an occasional weekly paper from Auburn, the growing little town north of Owasco Lake. At school, Mr. Castle allowed Millard to read Dwight's old geography of questions and answers. But without a map or atlas, he had just an obscure idea of how the world really looked.

By 1812, the New Hope school had improved and it owned a copy of Jedidiah Morse's geography, which Millard was allowed to borrow. He avidly devoured the impressions of the world contained in the precious book, especially James Bruce's travel to Abyssinia on the Red Sea. Images of it and other faraway places stayed with him day and night.

Millard was bright and quick to learn when there was the slightest opportunity. The weeks in school were so precious to him. But it frustrated Millard too. He felt he was forgetting as much as he was learning, and he was always so hungry for more book learning. He helped his father as best he could, but deep inside he couldn't shake the feeling that farming was not what he wanted for his

SOURCE DOCUMENT

THE

AMERICAN GEOGRAPHY;

OR, A

VIEW OF THE PRESENT SITUATION

OF THE

UNITED STATES OF AMERICA.

CONTAINING

Aſtronomical Geography; Geographical Definitions, Diſcovery, and General Deſcription

Of their Boundaries; Mountains; Lakes; Bays, and Rivers; Natural Hiſtory; Productions; Population; Government; Agriculture; Commerce; Manufactures; and Hiſtory.——A concife account of the War, and of the important Events which have ſucceeded:

A PARTICULAR DESCRIPTION OF

KENTUCKY, THE WESTERN TERRITORY, THE TERRITORY SOUTH OF OHIO, AND VERMONT;

Of their Extent; Civil Diviſions; Chief Towns; Climates; Soils; Trade; Character; Conſtitutions; Courts of Juſtice; Colleges; Academies; Religion; Iſlands; Indians; Literary and Humane Societies; Springs; Curioſities; Hiſtories; Mines; Minerals; Military Strength, &c.

WITH A VIEW OF THE

BRITISH, SPANISH, FRENCH, PORTUGUESE, AND DUTCH DOMINIONS, ON THE CONTINENT, AND IN THE WEST INDIES.

BY JEDIDIAH MORSE, A. M.

A NEW EDITION,

REVISED, CORRECTED, AND GREATLY ENLARGED, BY THE AUTHOR, *AND ILLUSTRATED WITH MAPS.*

LONDON:

PRINTED FOR JOHN STOCKDALE, PICCADILLY.

1794.

Though he longed to expand his knowledge, few books were available to Fillmore and the other students in the New Hope school. One of Fillmore's favorite books was Jedidiah Morse's Geography, shown here.

future. As he labored, he tried hard to remember what he had last learned, all the time picturing the places around the world about which he had read.

Tired of his father's poverty, Millard prayed for some opportunity to improve his station in life.

CHAPTER THREE

HANDLING THE ROWDIES

When Millard's Uncle Simeon moved west to the Niagara Frontier, he sent back news of the War of 1812. One evening a neighbor who had been drafted into the war visited Nathaniel to offer Millard a tidy sum of money to go as a substitute for him in the war.[1] Millard, who was by now a strapping young boy, was excited by the idea of being a powder boy. The thought of seeing more of the world than a little piece of Central New York was highly tempting to such a curious and ambitious boy.

Millard's mother and father wanted no part of this dangerous plan. Instead Nathaniel decided to arrange apprenticeships for his sons where the boys would go off to live with a master in a trade—such as carpentry, blacksmithing, weaving, or tinsmithing. They would work for almost free, usually spending seven years with the master tradesman, donating their labor in return for learning all the tricks of the trade. A life as a tradesman would be much better and easier than what Nathaniel knew to be the unreasonably hard life he had experienced as a pioneer farmer.

Mother Phoebe had had her fifth and sixth babies by now—Calvin in 1810 and Julia in 1812—and was soon to have her seventh. Millard's father knew that an apprenticeship would bring in about fifty-five dollars a year, and that hard-to-come-by cash would really help with his growing family. Millard was now fourteen years old, and it was time to start thinking about his future. Besides helping his future, an apprenticeship would keep this big, strong, growing boy fed and full.

In 1814 Benjamin Hungerford, a former neighbor of the Fillmores in New Hope and now a wool dresser in Sparta, returned to New Hope to buy wool and dyewoods. While in town, Hungerford called at the Fillmore home to see if Millard might be available as an apprentice.[2] Nathaniel arranged for Millard to return with Hungerford to Sparta as an apprentice—on a four-month trial. If it worked, the apprenticeship would probably last anywhere from four to seven years. Then Millard would be ready to begin his own business as a wool dresser, a master of such skills as cleaning, washing, and carding wool, then spinning, weaving, dyeing, and pressing the yarns and wools.

But the trip to Sparta held more adventures than the teenaged Millard had anticipated. Hungerford had driven an old team of horses to pull a heavy load back home on a very rutted road. To avoid putting extra weight on the wagon and tiring the horses, Millard was forced to walk

As a teenager Millard Fillmore was apprenticed to two wool dressers in New York. Millard learned to prepare and process wool into yarn and woven fabric.

a hundred miles across the state, past all the western Finger Lakes.[3]

Such a long, hard trek of several days left the poor homesick boy painfully tired, with sore feet and stiff limbs. To make matters worse, he was hungry because he was not used to the boiled salt pork and buckwheat cakes that Hungerford served. At home Millard had eaten bread and milk for nearly every meal.[4]

When Fillmore and Hungerford arrived, Hungerford's shop foreman, twenty-five-year-old William Scott, and the other apprentices came to assess the newest and youngest apprentice. Dressed in homespun sheep's-gray coat and trousers, a wool hat, and stout cowhide boots, Millard thoughtfully took in all the introductions. His chubby, ruddy face and bright eyes showed his intelligence and good nature. He gained the respect of the other apprentices immediately.

However, Hungerford's harsh speech and rough manner made Fillmore miss his kind father. Every mistake Millard made brought a humiliating outburst from Hungerford. Because Millard was the youngest of the apprentices, he was the one who had to chop all the wood for the fires under the many boiling kettles. Chop wood and nothing else for three months. Finally when Millard's frustration at not learning anything new could be contained no longer, he spoke up, telling Hungerford, "I could learn to chop wood at home and I am giving my time to learn a trade."[5]

The two had a heated argument. Millard could hear his father's constant words, "Do right," and had thought that all others he met in life would treat him with such integrity. He resolved that he would complete what he had promised for Mr. Hungerford, no matter what, and he continued to work in the shop, finishing up all of his promised time.

One day Millard and his new friend William Scott had to work until after dark. When they returned to Hungerfords' house, the family had eaten already and all the dishes had been used. After waiting for a while, Scott asked for clean bowls and spoons. Mrs. Hungerford looked at them crossly with her hands on her hips and said, "Well, suppose they have been used! Those that used them are decent people. I guess you needn't learn Millard to stick up his nose at our way of living. If the dishes on the table don't suit you, I can't help it!"[6]

All through December Millard longed to see more than little Sparta. He had seen no book, no newspaper, been to no church, and had no holiday until finally a New Year's Eve celebration came along. For the first time in his life, he saw the rough sports of the times—raffling, wrestling, whiskey drinking, and turkey shooting. Coerced into placing a bet to win a fat turkey, Millard won. Without a second thought, he put it back up for sale, pocketed the cash, and made one more resolution—never again to gamble a cent.[7]

At the end of the festivities, Millard and his fellow apprentices left together in the darkness of the January midnight. On the trip to the party, the path through the dark pine forest had not looked so foreboding, but now the mile-long path along a deep ravine was frightening. When the torch they carried with them went out, young Millard was nominated to be the one to go back to the party for a new light.

When he returned, he found his so-called friends had gone off together, leaving him to find his way alone. To make matters worse, a sudden and severe thunderstorm extinguished his light and left him in the darkest night he had ever seen. He held his hand out in front of his face and could not even see that.

Violent flashes of lightning revealed dense forest all around; thunder rolled terribly. At intervals he could hear the dashing waters of the stream below, swollen from the unseasonable rains and melted snow. He knew then that he was near the precipice, beneath which the water flowed. He hollered to his companions, who finally heard him and came back from the Hungerfords' with a light.

Another frightening event for Millard came when he was sent to Dansville to fetch some groceries. There were two or three inches of snow on the ground when Millard set out, and he almost enjoyed the chance to be off on his own, although he did notice that the route on which he had been sent seemed too roundabout. When he had finished the shopping, it was sundown, so he asked if there were a more direct way back to Sparta. He was told of an unfrequented path through a shrubby pine forest, which he took, easily following the fresh tracks of another person.

Just after dark, he was surprised to be stopped in his tracks by the slightly frozen Canaseraga Creek. A bridge had once crossed here, but no longer. Cobble abutments and one timber were all that remained of it now. Millard knew this ice was too thin to support him and the groceries. He could hear wolves howling in the distance, and he did not even have a stick to defend himself. He could also hear the crack of the ice breaking up from the rising flood.

Millard considered all his options. Then he climbed up on the cobble abutment, sat down on the skinny timber, and hitched himself across to safety.

Near the end of his promised four months, Millard was directed to prepare some blue dye, but somehow it came out wrong. When Hungerford yelled at him again, Fillmore decided it was time to go.

He packed up his few clothes and put some bread and dried venison in a knapsack. Happily he headed home, walking the hundred miles through the virgin forest all alone. The homecoming he received on that cold January night of 1815 when he opened a very familiar cabin door in New Hope was as warm as any hearth fire could ever be.

It was so good to be back home. Millard looked at his family now with a new appreciation. It surprised him to realize how tired and overworked his mother appeared. She always had such a sunny outlook on life, but the hardships of pioneer life were wearing down her health. Being the oldest son, Millard was only too happy to help out the family finances by taking another apprenticeship right near New Hope. He would be working again as a wool dresser, only this time for Zaccheus Cheney and Alvah Kellogg. The best part of this new arrangement was that Millard's father said he could work just half the year, from the beginning of June until Christmas, earning about fifty-five dollars, and he could go to school the rest of the year.

When Fillmore was seventeen, the town of Sempronius (of which New Hope was a part) established a small circulating library. Millard eagerly did any job to earn the extra two dollars—a large sum of money to him—so he could buy a share in the new library and become a member. Here a whole new world was opened to his hungry young mind. For the first time he was exposed to the history of his own nation, to the great works of Shakespeare, the adventures of Robinson Crusoe, and yes, even a map in which he could finally place all the names he remembered from Morse's *American Geography*. He read anything and everything, without any pattern or design. His biggest problem was in sneaking the time for such a luxury.

One big thing he was learning, however, was that he needed to improve his knowledge of the definitions of the words he was reading. After earning some extra money, Millard bought his very first book, a dictionary, and began his own program of seeking out the meaning of every new word from his reading. Even while he was at work at Cheney's factory, he would place his prized dictionary on the desk he passed by every two minutes. Then each time Millard had to feed the carding machines and remove the rolls, he would have a moment to look at a word, read its definition, and fix it in his memory. His vocabulary grew by leaps and bounds.[8]

In fact, his learning increased so quickly that people began to think of Millard as a teacher more than as a student. The winter he turned eighteen, Millard was employed to teach a country school in the town of Scott, south of Skaneateles Lake. The winter before, the rough boys there had driven out the teacher and broken up the school. He saw that the question of who was in charge had to be settled immediately. On the first day, of course, one of the boys challenged Fillmore's authority and tried to pick a fight. As if by a plan, the larger boys sprang to their feet to help their buddy. One even tried to grab the wooden poker by the wood stove. But Fillmore was too quick.

Raising the wooden poker himself and stamping his feet, he sternly told the ruffians to sit down. They obeyed. He punished the guilty instigator and the rest of the school day proceeded without further incident—until they all went home and the story started a bit of a breeze in the neighborhood.

A school meeting was called and Fillmore was asked

to attend. That was when he discovered that the boys' story had become a bit creative. They said that the new schoolmaster had used the poker to punish them. Fillmore calmly stated the facts and added that he was ready to quit if they desired it. But if he were to remain, he would be the master, even if he had to someday use the poker in self-defense. They all decided that school was to go on with Fillmore as the schoolmaster, and there was no further trouble.[9]

When the Scott school was closed for the growing season in the spring of 1818, Fillmore worked at a sawmill for a month or two. But he was eighteen and developing a strong case of wanderlust. In May he decided to visit his relatives on the Niagara Frontier. He walked one hundred forty miles, this time from Scott to Wales, a town southeast of Buffalo. His Uncle Calvin had moved west in 1807 with his wife Jerusha and had a sawmill in Lancaster. Earlier in the War of 1812, he had been a colonel whose company had been frequently called into service during the British invasions from Canada. Millard's three uncles, Elijah, Simeon, and Darius were also pioneering in western New York.

Millard saw the proof of the trouble caused by warfare when he first saw Buffalo. It was now four and a half years after the burning of Buffalo by the British. The city was just beginning to rise from the ashes, and there were many cellars and chimneys still without houses, showing the completeness of the destruction. It only matched the way that Millard now felt—his feet were blistered and every joint and muscle was intensely sore and aching from the long walk. He was bone tired from his nights on the cold hard ground.

This is what the port of Buffalo, New York looked like at the time of Fillmore's first visit there in 1818. Fillmore walked hundreds of miles during this journey.

Though exhausted, Millard left the young city. He crossed the Indian reservation to Aurora, along a long rotten causeway of logs extending across the low ground from Seneca Street nearly to the creek. After paddling himself over in a canoe borrowed from a friendly Indian, he stayed all night at an Indian tavern about six miles from Buffalo. It was not a good night's sleep though, with a crowd of drunken men keeping up a row most of the night. Early the next morning he walked alone through the woods to Willink and East Aurora, then into the town of Wales.[10]

After resting his blistered feet at the home of his relatives in Wales, he took off again to Geneseo, easily making a forty-mile trip in a day. For the first time, he saw the rich bottomlands of the Genesee River, and a few days later, the beautiful village of Canandaigua, which seemed to him to be an earthly paradise. Here he found stately homes, surrounded by trees, gardens, and orchards. Millard's eyes had been opened permanently to the possibility of life beyond the limits of his own farmer boy experiences.

CHAPTER FOUR

A REASON
TO ACHIEVE

In June of 1818 it was time for Fillmore to get back to his apprenticeship as a wool dresser at the Cheney mill, but every free minute found him with his nose in a book. He soon moved into Mr. Cheney's home so he could go to the new academy near Moravia. To pay his board, he promised to chop wood for two days for every week he lived there.

The extra effort was worth it. For the first time, he studied grammar and had the opportunity to study geography with a map.[1] Fillmore also met a lovely young lady named Abigail Powers. She had long black hair drawn tight to her head, large dark eyes, and a very gentle way about her. Although she was two years older than he was and of a higher social status, Abigail found a lot to admire in the serious, intelligent Fillmore. Of course, his strength and handsome good looks caught her eye too.

They happily spent the winter of 1819 in constant study together. Gradually they fell in love, but Fillmore knew now that he had to make something of himself to deserve the beautiful Abigail Powers as his wife. She was the sister of a judge and the daughter of a Baptist minister, the late Reverend Lemuel Powers.

But fate was at work. Fillmore's father had sold his tenancy and moved twelve miles southwest to Montville to be a tenant of the county judge, Walter Wood. Wood was a wealthy Quaker, and his law office thrived on land title lawsuits all over the Military Tract, just like the lawsuit that had stripped Millard's father of his first farm.[2] Nathaniel bragged to Judge Wood about his bright, well-read son and convinced the judge to try Millard out for two months as a law clerk.

At dinner, Phoebe was so excited with this secret that she just could hold it no longer and blurted out the splendid news to her son. Millard was completely overcome with the shock. He knew the study of law meant seven years of preparation without the benefit of a classical education, but he had to leave the table to hide his tears of joy. Perhaps this was the way he could earn the right to ask Abigail for her hand in marriage.

Bright and early the next morning, Fillmore reported to Judge Walter Wood for work. The quiet Quaker simply handed him the first law volume of *Blackstone's Commentaries* and said, "Thee will please turn thy attention to this."[3] Fillmore did, even though the legal language was hard to understand, especially without any explanation to accompany the reading. He finally copied one whole law book in order to learn all the mysteries hidden inside it.[4]

But he persevered and performed many errands for

the methodical judge. Fillmore studied to see what made this Quaker man such a success. He owned an impressive library, his energy seemed endless, and his punctuality was well known. He dressed plainly and spoke as a Quaker, using "thee" and "thy" for "you" and "your." He worked every day in the office from sun-up to 9 P.M., except when he attended the Quaker meeting twice a week.

When Fillmore's two-month apprenticeship as a law clerk had passed with very little encouragement from the judge, Millard sadly prepared to return to his apprenticeship at the mill. Gone were the hopes of position and security in a career of law. After packing his clothes, Millard stopped in the judge's offices to say thank you and farewell. However, Judge Wood spoke first.

> If thee has an ambition for distinction and can sacrifice everything else to success, the law is the road that leads to honors; and if thee can get rid of thy engagement to serve as an apprentice, I would advise thee to come again and study law.[5]

Fillmore's dashed hopes raced back to life, but as an apprentice whose promised time was not yet completed, he would have to buy his freedom. And he had no money to buy off his apprenticeship. Mr. Cheney had quit the mill to farm and his partner Kellogg needed more help than ever before at the mill. So Fillmore went back to the mill to fulfill his obligations. After another summer and fall of hard work, Mr. Kellogg agreed to let him go if he would relinquish his claim to last year's pay and pay an additional thirty dollars.

Judge Wood generously agreed to help out with this large amount of cash. The judge was a shrewd businessman and owned many farms spread over several counties.

SOURCE DOCUMENT

This letter from the Inspectors of Common Schools in New York gave Fillmore the certification necessary to teach school in the town of Sempronious.

He could use the help of this bright young man to both of their advantages.

Fillmore immediately took a teaching job in Sempronius, New York, for three winter months.[6] He earned some cash and borrowed one or two law books from Judge Wood to read in the early mornings and during the long cold evenings by candlelight. When his school closed in the spring, Fillmore went into Wood's office again and continued his studies until the next winter, a routine he repeated for many years. In the little spare time he had, he learned surveying, a skill that helped him to assist with the judge's many land holdings. This new skill provided him with yet another source of income.

After all, the young Mr. Fillmore had to set a new image now. He discarded his cowhide boots for a new pair of shoes, bought a new suit of homespun, and began to wear white collars and carry a cane. The people around Moravia were starting to notice this handsome six-foot tall young law clerk. For the Fourth of July celebration of 1821, Millard, now twenty-one, was asked to deliver a short address.[7]

Fillmore was jubilant to be learning the law, but he was also beginning to see the darker side of Judge Wood. One of the reasons he was so wealthy was because he was a cold-hearted businessman who evicted his tenants promptly when they were unable to pay, no matter the reason. And Fillmore was the one sent to do the dirty work.

One day, a farmer offered Millard three dollars to represent him in a suit before a justice of the peace. Millard agreed, but he cleverly masked his inexperience in the law by settling the case out of court. Judge Wood was furious when he learned what his apprentice had done. He ordered Fillmore not to practice before a justice of the peace again; he said it would ruin his legal language with justice-of-the-peace slang. Fillmore defended his actions and said he needed to earn some money of his own. Wood disagreed and insisted that Fillmore promise to never do it again.[8]

Slowly and sadly, Fillmore realized that the judge was more anxious to keep him dependent, to use him as a drudge in his business, than to make a lawyer out of him.

Again he knew that he was not being dealt with fairly. He thanked the judge for all his help, gave him a note saying he owed the judge the original thirty dollars plus thirty-five more, and left.[9]

Two years earlier Fillmore's mother and father had moved west to East Aurora, New York, to join their other relatives living there. His parents now owned a seventy-acre farm of their own in East Aurora, bought for $432 from the Holland Land Company. Millard decided to join them.

He still wanted nothing more than to be able to ask for Abigail Powers's hand in marriage, but first he knew he had to prove himself to her family. The Powers family considered Millard beneath them, since his father had been just a simple farmer. He would have to leave behind his beloved Abigail for now, but Millard hoped it would be just a year or two before he could finally propose to her. With four dollars in his pocket (three of it being his first legal fee from that fateful justice of the peace case), he retraced his journey of 1818, walking the one hundred forty miles alone and arriving in East Aurora at the end of the summer of 1821.

Quickly he took a teaching job in East Aurora to pay expenses. There was a little schoolhouse on Olean Road right near the main street. Uncle Calvin had moved to East Aurora in 1820 and owned a tavern around the corner on Main Street. He introduced his handsome young nephew to everyone. Millard even won a lawsuit for one of his relatives before a justice of the peace for a fee of four dollars. News spread that at last East Aurora had a lawyer, and Fillmore tried more and more cases on Saturdays.[10]

Teaching brought in about thirteen dollars a month (Fillmore was paid six dollars in cash and seven in grain). By the next winter, he was asked to teach about twenty East Aurora students from the beginning of October until February. The parents had collected $27.40 to pay him. This enterprising young man also earned about two dollars when he was surveying. It wasn't too long before he could repay his sixty-five dollar debt to Judge Wood, with interest.

In the spring of 1822, Millard bravely took a teaching job in the new Buffalo district school at Cold Spring for just one term. What a change in the city from a few years earlier! Buffalo was now a thriving community with a new harbor under construction. Erie Canal construction gangs were inching their way toward Buffalo and everyone knew that this canal would bring business to their shores, the western end of the canal. Shipyards and homes were springing up everywhere. Buffalo was now the busiest city in western New York, as busy as Millard Fillmore was.

He studied in a lawyer's office in the early morning, taught school during the day, and in the evening discussed the subject of the morning's study with a fellow student. He even worked in the post office, making up the mail routes and keeping the accounts of the office. It is no wonder that Buffalo's citizens took notice of this industrious and handsome new young man.[11]

Early in the summer of 1822, Fillmore's hard work and diligent study paid off. He passed the oral law exam, and with the recommendation of several prominent lawyers, he got an unpaid internship as a clerk in the Buffalo law office of Asa Rice and Joseph Clary. He continued to teach school in season to pay his expenses, but all his spare time was devoted to studying law.

In his clerkship, he had many opportunities to meet the leaders of this buzzing new city. He copied the way they spoke and their perfect style of dressing. The important citizens of Buffalo, in turn, noticed young Fillmore's serious attitude, sensible opinions, good manners, and careful way of living. But only twice did he have the time to walk all the way back to Moravia to keep alive his relationship with Abigail.

By the spring of 1823, after only twenty-seven months of studying law, Millard Fillmore was admitted to the bar to practice in the Court of Common Pleas. Because of his reputation for honesty, friendliness, and his quick mind for the law, he soon was offered a partnership in a well-known Buffalo law firm. He was even asked once again to fill in at the last moment for the missing Fourth of July speaker in Buffalo's remembrance celebration. During his oration, Fillmore spoke eloquently about the causes of the Revolution, the burning of Buffalo, and called for peace and harmony.[12]

It was time for Fillmore to carefully weigh all of his options. He knew, despite all his new popularity in Buffalo, that his grasp of the law still had some gaping holes in it. He finally decided to give up the prestigious job offer from the Buffalo law partnership and return to lawyer-less East Aurora.[13] Although it was not the bustling city that Buffalo had become, East Aurora was a pleasant little hamlet in a fertile valley with a sawmill and a gristmill on Cazenovia Creek, and a carriage shop and blacksmith shop on Main Street. Fillmore opened a small office in William Warren's office building on

In 1825 Fillmore built this law office (center) on Main Street in East Aurora, New York.

Olean Road near Main Street, right next to where he had taught school.

In East Aurora Fillmore had a monopoly on the petty legal business, such as handling documents for the Holland Land Company, mortgages, and collection of debts. He became one of East Aurora's leading citizens. By August 1824, he had saved enough money to build a law office on the north side of Main Street, right near his Uncle Calvin's tavern. It was a handsome little Greek Revival building with two fluted Doric columns for a touch of dignity. It was, after all, the first lawyer's office in town.

At long last in February, 1826, after eight years of courting Abigail, Millard finally felt important and promising enough to ask for her hand in marriage. He took a carriage to Moravia in the Finger Lakes and on the fifth of February, he and Abigail became man and wife. The marriage ceremony was held in the home of her prominent brother, Judge Cyrus Powers, and was performed by Reverend Orsanius Smith, who recorded it in the records of his church, St. Matthew's Episcopal. They were an old couple for those times, Abigail at twenty-eight and Millard at twenty-six. (Millard's younger brother Cyrus was married and had a child already.) But the new Mr. and Mrs. Fillmore had high goals for their lives, and theirs was a marriage for which they had been willing to wait.

For the first year or so, the young couple lived with Millard's parents in the farm on Olean Road so that Abigail could keep teaching school, this time at the East Aurora village school. And then Millard could begin to build a home for them.

In March of 1826, Millard bought the land right across the street from his law office on Main Street. His friends joined him in the excitement of building a little Greek Revival style house for East Aurora's most promising young man and his new bride.

Fillmore constructed the frame of their house from hand-hewn posts and beams, some with the bark still on the timbers. Millard fastened each connection with wooden pegs and laid the wide pine floors himself. Between each post he stretched and nailed split lath and then covered each wall with plaster. He even built Abigail a sturdy kitchen table from two wide wooden

This postcard shows the Fillmore home, built by Millard himself, on Main Street in East Aurora, just across the street from his law office.

planks cut from one of the giant trees that had grown near this pioneer village.

Abigail was a good sport to live the pioneer life for a spell, having left a much more civilized life behind in Moravia. But she kept herself busy with her teaching, even though most married women in those days stopped working outside the home as soon as they married. In the evenings, she and Millard studied law, literature, maps of ancient geography, and discussed all the issues of the day together. Learning and studying together was their greatest bond and shared joy.

Finally the little house was finished and they settled in on Main Street. Even then, Abigail kept on with her teaching, taking students who wanted to learn history into her keeping room for their lessons. Millard kept them both well supplied with books, writing often to his favorite bookstore in Albany for new additions to his library. Soon his personal library of one hundred fifty books equaled that of the town library started two years earlier by Uncle Calvin and his friends. Their home was filled with love and learning.

CHAPTER FIVE

ENTERING
POLITICS

Fillmore's Main Street home and law office quickly became the center of little East Aurora, New York. In the cold winter months, Fillmore studied and worked at his large law office desk, wearing a black quilted robe for warmth and a green tinted eyeshade, an open-topped visor that lessened his eye strain while reading. Friends and neighbors felt free to interrupt him and often stopped by for a chat by the fireplace with Fillmore. And the only recreation in East Aurora during long summer evenings was to gather on the front step of Fillmore's office and listen to the stories of all the townsfolk. Everyone stopped by to hear Millard's stories of what was going on in all the important towns he had visited to conduct his business—from Mayville to Batavia to Canandaigua. The residents of East Aurora enjoyed hearing the news from these other towns.

Fillmore befriended Nathan Hall, a motherless boy who had moved west to Wales Center from Skaneateles, New York. He was ten years younger than Millard, but at sixteen he became a law student under Fillmore. Like Fillmore had in his law student phase, Hall taught school during the winter months and surveyed land whenever anyone asked him to do the work.

On one evening, a young East Auroran named George Johnson turned to Fillmore suddenly and asked, "Fillmore, why don't you get into Congress and get profitable positions for Hall and me?" Everyone laughed. But Millard paused and said seriously, "Stranger things than that have happened, Johnson."[1]

The Fillmores brought with them to East Aurora a search for education and intellectual stimulation that was contagious. Before long, all the prominent young men of East Aurora got together and formed the Aurora Union Debating Society. Every week or so a dozen or more men congregated at a chosen location, picked sides, and debated questions like "Have women more influence over men than wine?" (they decided "yes"), and "Is the drunkard a greater nuisance to society than the profane swearer?" ("no"—obviously this was decided before the days of cars.) On March 31, 1825, the question was, "Is fire a more powerful element than water?" Fillmore said no and his side won. The next week on April 7th, they debated, "Is it right to take life for any crime?" Fillmore said no, and on this issue, he lost.[2]

Fillmore was caught up in Buffalo's excitement over the coming Erie Canal, a waterway financed by the state of New York that would link New York Harbor with the Great Lakes. He was East Aurora's representative in the

SOURCE DOCUMENT

The records of the Aurora Union Debating Society, a young men's club that Fillmore joined in East Aurora, show that the April 7, 1825 debate was about crime and punishment and whether it was permissible to take the life of a criminal.

campaign to connect this new canal with the Allegheny River by building a North-South Canal. This could then connect with the Mississippi River system. But the Erie Canal ended up being the last of the great canals to be built in western New York. It was finally opened—after eight long years of hard labor—in October, 1825, with a procession of boats from Buffalo to New York City. New York Governor Dewitt Clinton celebrated with a ceremony known as "wedding the waters." He poured two red-white-and-blue kegs of Lake Erie water into the harbor of the Atlantic Ocean. A month later a keg of ocean water was sent to Buffalo to be dumped into the fresh waters of Lake Erie.

Fillmore's Uncle Calvin had taken the plunge into New York state politics by winning the race for state assemblyman in 1825. His example showed Fillmore that it was an easy time for ordinary men to get involved in politics and make a difference in the development of the western New York frontier. Millard got involved in what became known as the "Agrarian Movement," helping landowners fight for lower land prices and lower mortgage and interest rates from the powerful Holland Land Company.

Once again, on the Fourth of July—a special one since America was fifty years old in 1826—Millard Fillmore was the featured speaker at East Aurora's Independence Day celebration. He was eloquent, talking about liberty, self-government, equality, and tyranny. He did not know that within three months an event would take place that would change the whole course of his life.

In September of 1826 in Batavia, New York, a man named William Morgan wrote a booklet revealing the

Masonic symbols, shown in this chart, include the all seeing eye, ark, beehive, lamb, globes atop columns, square and compass, trowel, and anchor. The Anti-Masonic Party rose in opposition to what was perceived as the secrecy and conspiracy of the fraternal order of Freemasonry.

secrets of a fraternal society know as the Freemasons, or Masons. Morgan was a member of this secretive society, which brought men together based on a common set of beliefs. Angered by Morgan's publication, the master of the nearby Canandaigua Masonic Lodge got a warrant to arrest Morgan for an outstanding two-dollar debt he owed. A group of Masons then abducted Morgan, who was never seen alive again. The Masons were widely believed to have murdered him.

The "Morgan affair," as the incident became known, intensified existing anti-Masonic feelings in New York as well as other parts of the country. Because the Masons were an elite group whose members included most public officeholders, many felt that the order wielded too much influence. In the case of William Morgan's disappearance, anti-Masonics accused the prosecutors in the case and others of being involved in a conspiracy to cover up a crime committed by their fellow Masons.

Many preachers condemned the Masons from their pulpits; some even refused to serve communion to men who were known to be Masons. The big issue was not the Mason's secrecy, but which law was higher—that of the United States Constitution or that of the Freemasons. The anti-Masonic crusade soon grew into a political movement. A smart young Rochester newspaperman by the name of Thurlow Weed named his paper the *Rochester Anti-Masonic Enquirer* and fanned the flames of indignation even higher. Weed was a staunch backer of President John Quincy Adams, whose chief opponent for the election of 1828 was Andrew Jackson. Weed was happy to point out that Jackson was a Mason, and he hoped this fact would help put John Quincy Adams back into the presidency.

Fillmore joined those in his circle in East Aurora who were angry at the twisting of justice in the Morgan affair. He didn't have anything against the Masons, but he felt that the nation's laws must be held higher than the rules of any lesser organization. He made up his mind that something must be done so that a person could not be thrown into prison for owing a measly two dollars. There had been times in the not too distant past when he had owed much more than that.

In 1827, Fillmore earned the title of attorney of the state supreme court. With this new office he traveled even more, meeting influential people and encountering larger issues all the time. In 1828, he was a county delegate for the first statewide convention of the new Anti-Masonic Party. Led by Thurlow Weed, the party had mobilized support throughout the state.

Weed and Fillmore met for the first time at the 1828 Anti-Masonic convention. Weed was at the beginning of his career as a political boss, in which he controlled the outcomes of elected politics from behind the scenes. He admired the young, well-spoken lawyer from western New York and began to convince Fillmore to run for elective office.

Weed saw the potential in Fillmore. He had been born in a log cabin, just like Andrew Jackson, who was now running for president of the United States for the second time. It was the era of the common man. Fillmore was tall, handsome, and serious; he had many friends and a great reputation. He also had a beautiful, intelligent wife and a child on the way.

Eighteen hundred and twenty-eight was a turning point for the new couple. On April 25th Millard and Abigail became parents to a son, Millard Powers Fillmore. To avoid confusion with two Millards in the house, they called their son "Powers."

Fillmore also attended a Democratic-Republican convention held in Erie County, New York, in May of 1828, where he found himself deeply involved in Weed's sticky political maneuvers. The group chose John Quincy Adams for their presidential candidate and Fillmore voted each time the way Weed wanted him to. Fillmore came away as both the Democratic-Republican and the Anti-Masonic candidate for state assemblyman.

Fillmore won his first election with more votes than any other candidate in the county, and he became a New York state assemblyman. But the Democratic-Republican presidential candidate, John Quincy Adams, lost the presidential election. Instead, Andrew Jackson was elected the next president of the United States.

Many trips to Albany, New York's capital, were required of new state assemblyman Fillmore. Abigail continued teaching in her front room at the house in East Aurora, even with little Powers and her own home to care for. She was lonely for her husband and wrote to him every day while he was away on business.

Fillmore used his time in Albany well, studying the process of passing laws. Mindful of the unfair treatment of William Morgan, by his second year he had written a law abolishing prison terms for those who could not pay debts. To make his law successful, he had to spend many hours in research and pay attention to details. The challenge was to please both sides of the issue. In Fillmore's law, debtors got freedom from jail, which was popular among the common man, while the business world got a new state bankruptcy law included in the deal. Fillmore made his name in Albany by succeeding with the passage of this law. Other states even copied this bill. Soon, all over the nation, thousands of debtors were joyously released from prisons to go home and work to pay their debts.

Fillmore also helped to allocate state money for the relief of paupers, even though there were none in East Aurora. His hometown received money to improve important bridges and obtained permission to sell the old East Aurora schoolhouse for thirty-four dollars because it was located in too noisy a spot near the business center. He knew that well as a former schoolteacher there.

Success had finally come to the former tenant farmer's son. Fillmore was enjoying his new family, home, and political influence.

CHAPTER SIX

FILLMORE, HALL, AND HAVEN

Millard and Abigail agreed it was time to join the larger arena of Buffalo, so Fillmore became a member of the law firm of Joseph Clary, where he had clerked eight years earlier. In May of 1830, Fillmore rented his little house out and bought a building lot on Tuscarora Street, now known as Franklin Street, just two blocks west of Main Street in Buffalo. From there, he could easily walk to work.

On this lot, builders constructed a simple two-story, six-room Federal style white clapboard house where Fillmore would live for the next twenty-five years. It was like Fillmore—strong, handsome, and quietly tasteful. The house had five bay windows trimmed with green shutters and a center hall entrance, featuring a staircase with a handsome rosewood banister. On the left was the

Fillmores' library, lined with filled bookcases. Millard already had accumulated a large collection of books.

He was known never to go to New York City without bringing home a few books with him, followed or preceded by a package sent by express with even more books. When the overflow of books exceeded Abigail's shelf space, she would have a new section built on the bookcases.[1] As if to make up for all the reading he missed as a child, all of Millard's leisure time was spent poring over his books.

In 1830, the city of Buffalo was a funnel, sending out to the new frontiers of Michigan and Illinois thousands of European immigrants who had traveled there from New York City by way of the Erie Canal. The population of the city more than doubled in the 1830s, from 8,000 to 18,000. Native Americans from the nearby Buffalo Creek reservation walked through the streets in their blankets and moccasins. Neighborhood hogs and cows roamed the mud roads, grazing on any front yards that were unprotected by fences.[2]

Millard and Abigail were smarter than that. They put up a neat white fence within which Abigail designed, planted, and tended one of the most beautiful flower gardens in Buffalo. In the front yard she planted lilacs and Japanese quince bushes.

The weather of Buffalo created a four-month social season every winter. The harbors of Lake Erie closed over with ice, so shipping was impossible. Business, therefore, was conducted for the other eight months and shut down every winter.

The Fillmores were ready for this new and exciting social life—formal dinners and dances, Shakespearean plays at the Eagle Street Theatre, chamber music recitals, and visiting lecturers and celebrities such as the editor and publisher Horace Greeley. There was the Fireman's Ball, the Military Ball on Washington's Birthday, and the Civic Ball in the ballroom of the American Hotel.[3]

Fillmore's gallant manners impressed the ladies of Buffalo. As soon as he and Abigail arrived at one winter party, he suddenly remembered the flower arrangement that Abigail had prepared as a hostess gift and forgotten. Without telling Abigail, he made sure she was all settled in the parlor, then quietly slipped back home to fetch the flowers so as not to upset her.[4]

Fillmore was soon appointed to a committee that persuaded the state legislature to incorporate Buffalo as a city. The governor of New York approved the incorporation in April 1832, and Buffalo soon began a system of fire protection, building four reservoirs to hold water for fire fighting. Fillmore also helped to form the Buffalo Mutual Fire Insurance Company.

As former teachers and avid students, the Fillmores saw a great need to improve the public education system in Buffalo and to establish a library. They promptly joined the Lyceum, a local study group designed to educate adults with lectures, formal debates, and chemistry and physics experiments. The members of the Lyceum collected documents, books, rocks, plants, and objects of art. They kept a reading room and library and worked to build better public schools. Fillmore soon became vice president of the Lyceum.

Abigail Fillmore had a lifelong quest for learning. She taught herself to speak French, and when she had mastered it well enough to be able to read and translate

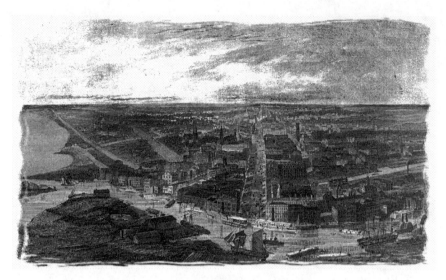

A nineteenth century view of Buffalo, New York. Millard and Abigail Fillmore moved to this bustling city in 1830.

easily, she took up piano playing. She read avidly and was very well informed on all the issues that her husband had to consider as a lawmaker. In fact, said a close friend, "Millard never took any important step without her counsel and advice."[5]

The Fillmores also became charter members of the First Unitarian Society of Buffalo, which was located just a few hundred yards from their home. The young couple chose the Unitarian belief because of its emphasis on reason. Sunday was absolutely honored as a day of rest in the Fillmore home.

Their fellow parishioner, Oliver Steele, began a free common school system in Buffalo, supported by city taxes and controlled by the city government. It was the first community in New York State to establish free, tax-supported elementary schools. The Fillmores had been among his strongest supporters for eight years in this important step for the city of Buffalo.

In 1831 Fillmore took his assembly seat for the third time in Albany. Sadly, his mother Phoebe died that year at the young age of forty-nine. Millard was happy that he had been able to pay many visits to her as she reached her last days. She had lived a hard life as a pioneer woman, raised nine children, and was deeply loved by all.

Great joy came to the Fillmore family on March 27, 1832, when Abigail and Millard became the parents of a daughter, Mary Abigail, known as "Abby." She was a ray of sunshine right from the moment she was born.

But that spring the news that paralyzed Buffalo was the great fear that cholera was coming their way. The killer disease had progressed from Europe to Quebec, and was traveling down the St. Lawrence River. In terror the Fillmores read of 3,500 deaths from cholera in New York City, and 5,000 in New Orleans in just two weeks. Cholera came to Buffalo in the heat of July and took two hundred to their deaths. Millard and Abigail had wisely packed up their children to go live with Grandpa Nate in East Aurora for the summer. The Fillmores had escaped the clutches of cholera this time. But the alarming disease would strike twice in their future.

In the fall of 1832 Fillmore took several important steps. Running as an Anti-Masonic, he was elected to the U.S. House of Representatives in Washington, D. C. Then he left his partnership with Joseph Clary to start his own law firm with Nathan Hall, his former student. Nathan had married Abigail's friend Emily Paine and bought a house just a few doors away from the Fillmores.

The Fillmore & Hall law office was a second story

SOURCE DOCUMENT

Washington Dec. 22. 1833.
Sunday. afternoon.

My Dear Son,

       I send to you in this letter, a little book which will tell you about a gold ring.
         You must read it all through to your ma. — and be a good boy and go to school, and learn to read and write, so as to write a letter to your pa.
        I am your
           Affectionate
             Father

               M. Fillmore.

M.P. Fillmore:

While serving in Washington, D.C. as a U.S. representative from New York, Fillmore wrote this letter home to his young son, Powers.

office up steep steps on the west side of Main Street. The office was lit by sperm oil lamps and warmed by two cast iron wood-burning stoves. Hung on a clothes tree in Fillmore's office were his two black quilted robes, a heavy one for the winter and a light one for the summer. As in East Aurora, he always wore his green eyeshade when studying his books and papers. And Fillmore loved serving as a teacher again with his student-clerks.

One of the first issues Millard had to face as a representative in Washington was a pile of petitions from abolitionists who wanted Congress to ban slavery in the nation's capitol. Right in the Washington Mall next to the Smithsonian Castle was a slave auction business. Fillmore presented a similar petition from the people of Rochester and voted in favor of Congress's receiving these petitions, but the majority of congressmen threw them out. This infuriated those who considered the right of the people to petition as essential to a democracy.

After his two-year term was up in 1835, Millard took two years off from public service to take in a new law partner, Solomon Haven, who became Buffalo's best trial lawyer. The firm of Fillmore, Hall & Haven became known all over the state, the eastern seaboard, and even in the West. All three men attended the Unitarian Church, lived in the same neighborhood, and socialized together often. All three were self-made men, without the benefit of fancy education, wealth, or powerful connections.

More Fillmore family losses came when Millard's brother Darius, a young law student, died of consumption in East Aurora. Millard's brother Almon, also an aspiring lawyer, had died earlier in 1830. Millard's sisters Julia and Phoebe Maria came to live with Millard and Abigail in Buffalo. Both were planning to teach schools in Aurora. Meanwhile Abigail lost three of her older brothers. Millard's father, however, had found a new wife in the widow Eunice Love.

During this time Fillmore helped Thurlow Weed convince the Anti-Masonics to transfer their allegiance to a new political party known as the Whigs. Unbeknownst to Fillmore, this was the party that would take him all the way to the Oval Office.

CHAPTER SEVEN

LEADER OF
THE WHIGS

Just as Fillmore returned to Congress in 1837 as a Whig, another war with Great Britain was threatening Buffalo. Canadian rebels seeking independence from Britain had enlisted the support of sympathetic Americans who sent the privately owned American steamer *Caroline* to assist in the rebel uprising. Canadian militia who were loyal to Britain later set the *Caroline* on fire and sent it over Niagara Falls, killing those on board, including an American citizen. Angry Americans demanded that the United States seek justice against Britain. But President Martin Van Buren sought to avoid another war.

As the congressman from Buffalo, Fillmore urged Congress not to react with threats, but to build up more troops on the northern border. "I would submit that the best way to avoid a war with Great Britain is to show her that we are prepared to meet her, if there is to be a war; because reasonable preparations for defense are better than gasconading [boasting]."[1]

Millard also asked for an iron vessel to be built in Buffalo for the Great Lakes. As a result, Congress voted more money to strengthen Buffalo and the mighty man-of-war *Michigan* was built as well.[2] The merchants of Buffalo were also ecstatic that Fillmore had convinced Congress to spend money expanding Buffalo's harbor.

At thirty-eight, Fillmore was now nationally known and respected. He was tall and strong from his years of splitting wood on the frontier. His handsome kind face inspired trust.

Following the 1838 congressional elections, a controversy arose over the disputed election of five New Jersey congressmen. The outcome of this dispute would determine which party was the majority—the Democrats or the Whigs—and who would have control of the House of Representatives. A committee was chosen to solve the problem, but somehow the Democrats made sure that all five committee members were Democrats. An angry Fillmore tried to read a minority report into the records. But the Democratic Speaker of the House stopped him. Then Fillmore gave one of the most passionate speeches of his life, warning that the majority was acting dangerously in silencing the minority, since the same treatment could be used against them someday. For now, the Democrats got their way.

The biggest issue and deepest scar in the country at this time was the institution of slavery. Many people in the North thought it unconscionable that southerners kept slaves. Gradually the abolition movement grew into

Mary Abigail "Abby" Fillmore.

a very strong force. Abolitionists thrived in western New York, and many of them helped runaway slaves escape to freedom in Canada. The first antislavery party in the United States, the Liberty Party, was organized in Warsaw, New York, in 1839.

The Anti-Slavery Society of Erie County wrote a letter to Fillmore when he was up for re-election in 1838, asking his stand on slavery issues. He answered back that yes, he was opposed to all slavery but made no pledges on votes. "Please rely on my character to legislate correctly. . . On every important subject, I deliberate before action, to possess all information, listen to every argument and then I vote."[3]

Another troublesome issue was the amazing number of immigrants coming into America—six hundred thousand between 1830 and 1840 alone. Congressman Fillmore was especially concerned because so many immigrants settled in Buffalo at the end of the Erie Canal. Canal Street was an infamous neighborhood whose crime and poverty worried concerned citizens like the Fillmores. Many were afraid that these newcomers would not understand the issues and democracy for which Americans had fought. Since so many new immigrants were Catholic, native-born citizens worried that the Pope in Rome would control their votes. Worse yet, they feared that immigrants would vote the way a tricky politician told them to. Some New York City Whigs even started a Nativist, or "Know-Nothing," Party to fight against immigrants.

But in 1840, the Whigs celebrated the election of the first Whig president of the United States—William Henry Harrison. Fillmore had helped campaign for Harrison and he was rewarded with the job of chairman of the Ways and Means Committee, a powerful Congressional committee. In this job, Fillmore met inventor Samuel Morse, the son of American geographer Jedidiah Morse. Morse had patented his electric telegraph and was exhibiting it in Washington. Fillmore saw the importance of this invention, and using his position as chairman of the Ways and Means Committee, he secured thirty thousand in funds to construct an electric telegraph from Washington to Baltimore. A year later in the U.S. Supreme Court room in the Capitol, Morse tapped out his famous message on the telegraph, "What hath God wrought!"[4]

Harrison had promised to toe the Whig line, standing for business interests— decent highways to deliver goods, a protective tariff to keep imports from beating out the prices of U.S.-made products, and a national banking system. The joy of finally having a Whig president did not last, though, for Harrison died suddenly just a month after his inauguration, the first president to die in office. Vice President John Tyler took office as president in 1841 and soon revealed that his true political leanings were not really Whig, but Democratic.

Tyler fought against tariffs, but Fillmore delivered a famous speech for the Tariff Law of 1842, a law he had written. He wanted to protect American industry to build an American spirit and cultivate a deeper feeling of nationality. Tyler was finally forced to sign Fillmore's tariff into law.

Fillmore chose not to run for Congress in 1842, even though he was re-nominated. He needed time for his thriving law business. Fillmore had also had enough of serving under President Tyler, who opposed everything the Whig Congress tried to do. It felt like warfare every day in Congress.[5] Powerful Senator Henry Clay of Kentucky had left the Senate because he also clashed with Tyler. Fillmore was even talked about as a possible running mate with Clay on the 1844 Whig presidential ticket.

But at the 1844 Whig convention in Baltimore, Thurlow Weed worked some back-room politics. By now, Fillmore had learned not to trust Weed, and sure enough, Weed blocked Fillmore's chance to run as vice president by having him nominated for governor of New York.

With all the abolitionists and the many Irish, Dutch, and German immigrants voting against the Whigs, Fillmore lost badly in the 1844 gubernatorial election. It was the first time Fillmore had ever lost an election, and he held it against immigrants and Thurlow Weed for the rest of his life. "All is gone but honor," he sadly said, but in some ways he was glad not to have to take on state policy.[6] His specialty was national politics. Meanwhile, a Democrat, James Knox Polk, became the next president of the United States.

Fillmore was now able to devote more time to his family. Young Powers had grown to be an extremely shy young man. His parents had a hard time coaxing him to enter a room with anyone other than family in it. Abby was an outgoing, bright child. Both children attended public schools in Buffalo. Abby busily studied German, Spanish, French, and Italian with private tutors. She also mastered drawing, painting of botanical prints, piano, and harp. She was as anxious to learn as her parents, and she had all the opportunities that Fillmore had missed as a youth.

The Fillmores wanted their children to be useful members of society. They paid a lot of attention to their early schooling, trained them to work, and taught them about duty to others.

Powers attended the Law School at Albany and went on to Harvard Law School at Cambridge.[7] Abby studied at the select family school of Mrs. Sedgwick in Lenox, Massachusetts, for a year and then graduated with the highest honors after six months at the State Normal School for teachers.

By 1844 Powers was working as a law clerk at

Fillmore & Haven, along with a promising young man named Hiram Day. Both Fillmore and Haven worked until ten at night and the students were expected to be there, either reading or copying law. The law apprentices swept the office, built the fires, and filled and trimmed the lamps. They delivered letters to the post office two or three times a day.

Once a week at 7:15 P.M., an exam would be held, with Millard seated in his office in his swivel chair, his two lamps burning behind him. His five students sat in a half circle in front of their master. Millard asked each about his reading and asked if there were any questions, leading into a group discussion. The sessions adjourned around 10:30 at night, providing a very pleasant and effective learning experience.

He also held high standards for his students. "Last evening as I was taking a ride with Mrs. Fillmore," Fillmore told Day, "we saw you and Powers walking out on Main Street and going as though you were walking on a wager [racing to win a bet]; that is undignified and unprofessional."[8]

Once the railroad to western New York was completed in 1840, Niagara Falls became the summer resort for the whole country and many famous people stopped by the Fillmore & Haven office to visit. In October, 1843, the Fillmores entertained John Quincy Adams, the former president and now an esteemed congressman. Millard and Abigail had a small circle of friends over to meet Mr. Adams and all enjoyed a remarkable conversation. They also took him to services at their church, since he too was a Unitarian. Adams left with the compliment: "Millard Fillmore was one of the ablest, most faithful and fairest-minded men with whom it has been my lot to serve in public life."[9]

In 1846, Fillmore joined with several Buffalo doctors to found the University of Buffalo, which began as a medical college. When the doctors couldn't get a charter from the Board of Regents, Fillmore called on his old partner, Nathan Hall, then a state assemblyman from Buffalo. Hall saved the day by passing a special bill that created the university. Fillmore was chosen to be the first chancellor of the university, an office he held until he died. He enjoyed attending lectures, chatting with students, and presiding at commencements.

A highlight for Abigail during these years was the Leland family reunion. Her father's mother, Thankful Leland, was from this powerful family, and the gathering drew one or two thousand. What a thrill it was for Abigail to enter the reunion with the glow of triumph on her cheeks. Her husband, whom some of her family and friends said she should not marry, was now a well-known name in every home of New York State. It was an event that Millard and Abigail talked about with pleasure for years.[10]

But Fillmore's political life was not so blissful. He and Thurlow Weed were feuding again. Fillmore backed the opponent to Weed's candidate for New York governor, and Weed was furious when Fillmore's candidate won. But in 1847 they patched up their relationship long enough for Fillmore to win the New York state comptroller job. He was the first person elected to this important position, which put him in charge of the state's finances. He won election with the largest vote any New York Whig had ever received.

Fillmore sold his law books to Solomon Haven, now the mayor of Buffalo, and closed down the firm of Fillmore & Haven. Since both Powers and Abby were in school in Massachusetts, he and Abigail moved in December, 1847, to an Albany temperance hotel, where no alcohol was allowed. This was the first time that Abigail had moved out of Buffalo since 1830. She was not as healthy as could be, and hotel living made her life much easier.

Fillmore used his time as state comptroller to improve and enlarge the canal system of New York. He also revised the state's banking code in a system that combined the lightness and convenience of paper currency with the security of gold and silver. It was so effective that the whole country adopted this currency system sixteen years later.[11]

One day when Fillmore was talking with the secretary of state in the comptroller's office, a baseball crashed through the window and landed at his feet. The boys responsible simply pulled out another ball and continued their game, until a tall gentleman appeared in the west door of the state hall with their baseball in his hand. The boys froze in awe and fear, but Fillmore just gently tossed the ball back, bowed, and disappeared, leaving the boys feeling very lucky.

Another war, this time with Mexico, began to heat up the national climate. President Polk declared war in 1846 when Mexicans fired on U.S. soldiers, killing eleven. He sent General Zachary Taylor, known as "Old Rough and Ready," to invade Mexico, resulting in a huge gain in territory that would eventually become the states of New Mexico, Colorado, Utah, Arizona, Nevada, and California.

Fillmore was selected as the Whig's vice presidential candidate in 1848.

General Taylor became a national hero and soon Thurlow Weed was grooming him to run for president. Taylor said he had no qualifications for the job, which was true, but he was willing. Since Taylor was a plantation owner with over a hundred slaves, the southern Whigs considered him an excellent candidate.

In June of 1848, Weed had Taylor nominated at the Whig convention in Philadelphia, where he won out over more logical and qualified candidates like Daniel Webster, Henry Clay, and another Mexican War hero, General Winfield Scott. Clay had already had two tries at the presidency. But Taylor was the new face in town, and he won the heated race on the fourth ballot.

When Taylor won the Whig nomination, a northern delegate jumped up onto a table and announced that the choice of this southerner marked the end of the Whig Party. Another Whig, John Collier, quickly stood and proclaimed that he was a Clay supporter and against slavery, but he would support Taylor if he had a vice president who would heal the rift between the slavery and antislavery delegates. He suggested Millard Fillmore for vice president. Since Taylor was from the South, the Whigs felt the ticket should be balanced with a vice president from the North. Millard won the nomination in only two ballots, infuriating Weed who had wanted his old favorite, William Seward, as vice president.[12]

Even though slavery was the hot issue of the day, both the Democrats and the Whigs avoided discussing it in the campaign of 1848.

Fillmore felt that the national government should not take an active role in opposing slavery. He had always regarded slavery as an evil, but he thought that the Constitution allowed individual states to decide whether to permit or ban slavery.

Back in his home state and in his hometowns of East Aurora and Buffalo, there was strong antislavery senti-ment, and the Underground Railroad flourished. This secret network was made up of whites and free blacks who willingly broke the law to help slaves find freedom. Each stop on the "railroad" had different ways to hide the fugitives—secret rooms in the basement or thick haylofts in the barn—until a "conductor" smuggled them onto the next "station," perhaps hiding them in a horse-drawn cart or wagon. The last station was Black Rock, north of Buffalo, where the swift Niagara River is the narrowest. Federal marshals and bounty hunters lurked there on the riverfronts, looking for fugitive slaves. Many Black Rock residents were involved in the Underground Railroad, and some served the agents whiskey or distracted them with rowdy songs. Others rowed slaves across the Niagara in skiffs, silently providing a ferry ride to Canada. Halfway over, the slaves were free.

The Whigs won easily in November 1848, especially with the electoral votes New York provided. So in February, two weeks before his inauguration as vice president of the United States, Fillmore resigned as New York comptroller and moved to Washington, D.C. Abigail and Abby returned to Buffalo for the time being, since Powers had just begun a law practice there and Abby was hoping to get a teaching job. Or perhaps it was because sixteen-year-old Abby was already being courted by the young lawyer in her father's office, Hiram Day. Hiram had grown to love the vivacious and beautiful Abby, and knowing her love for music, gifted her with a beautiful harp and a candle-lit music stand.

But her mother Abigail's health and spirits were not good. Her beloved older sister Mary had died in 1848 at fifty-five, a loss Abigail could almost not bear. She wrote Fillmore every day, urging him to visit her whenever he could. After her fiftieth birthday, she had a premonition that she might not see many more birthdays herself. The Fillmores had tragedy ahead of them.

CHAPTER EIGHT

THE THIRTEENTH PRESIDENT

On Thursday, the Fourth of July of 1850, President Taylor attended the celebrations at the newly-begun Washington Monument. It was a broiling hot day and Taylor soon collapsed from sunstroke. The next morning he was ill with a raging fever. On Monday Vice President Fillmore joined those holding a vigil outside the president's bedroom. At noon on Tuesday, Fillmore adjourned the Senate to hurry back to the White House. By the night of July 9th, Taylor was dead from cholera.

That night was the only sleepless night of Fillmore's life, so overwhelmed was he by the great responsibilities ahead of him.[1] Unlike Taylor, he knew what an enormous job the presidency was and what difficulties the nation faced. He wrote to his Buffalo minister, Reverend Hosmer, about the serious earnestness with which he took up his

Millard Fillmore took the presidential oath on July 10, 1850, one day after President Taylor's death.

great duty. He said how deeply he felt his dependence upon God and with all his heart sought His guidance.[2] Fillmore also sent a gracious message to President Taylor's widow, encouraging her to take as long as she needed to remain in the White House.

At noon on Wednesday, July 10th, Fillmore took the oath of office before a joyless Congress. He became the second man to inherit the presidency through death.

But Fillmore had no time to savor his new office. On the night of Taylor's death, the entire cabinet had resigned, rather than serve under the man that Weed and Seward had taught them to despise. Fillmore refused to consider their resignations until Taylor was buried. Then he asked them to remain for a month; they gave him a week.

Within two weeks, Fillmore had chosen a whole new cabinet. It was made up of three northerners, two southerners and two men from border states—all of them dedicated to preserving the Union and all favoring compromise to do so. Fillmore's friend Nathan Hall became Postmaster General, just as their friend George Johnson had predicted way back in East Aurora.

There was no honeymoon period for the new president. Henry Clay's Compromise, a valiant effort to keep the nation from dividing over the issue of slavery, was voted down in July. Because Fillmore had listened to all the arguments in building the compromise, he understood the complexities involved. He felt it was time for him to act to heal the strife in the country. Fillmore put the full support of his administration behind the measure, which was brought before Congress again and passed. Abigail predicted that signing the compromise would be Fillmore's political death. Fillmore was no friend of slavery, but he believed in the Constitution, which allowed slavery, and in the union of the states. "We have received from our fathers a Union and a constitution above all price and value," Fillmore said,

> and he is unworthy of his country who cannot sacrifice everything for their support . . . I well knew, that by so doing, I must lose the friendship of many men . . . especially in my own state, and encounter their reproaches . . . to me, this is nothing. The man who can look upon a crisis without being willing to offer himself upon the altar of his country is not fit for public trust.[3]

An incident at this time revealed Fillmore's personal feelings about slavery. His presidential coachman, a free black man named William Williams, confided to Fillmore during a ride that his wife, three daughters and three grandchildren—all slaves—had been put up for sale at midnight on August 2, 1850. They had been kidnapped and were imprisoned in a slave pen in Baltimore, waiting to be shipped to New Orleans.[4]

When Fillmore heard the story, he got out of the carriage, gave Williams cash to go to Baltimore to learn

SOURCE DOCUMENT

SLAVERY AND THE SLAVE TRADE IN THE DISTRICT OF COLUMBIA.

Congress, by the Constitution of the United States, has the right " *to exercise exclusive legislation, in all cases whatsoever,*" over the District of Columbia.—*See* Constit. U. S. Art I. Sect. 8.

Under the authority of Congress, and therefore of the whole people of the United States, more than SIX THOUSAND men, women and children are held as SLAVES in this District.

Under the same authority, a slave-trade, as atrocious as any known in the world, is carried on in the same District. Slave Factories, with *chains and grated cells,* are established at the Seat of Government, where slaves are constantly collecting from the neighboring States, and thence regularly shipped in cargoes, or sent, *literally manacled together, in droves,* to the more remote South. The Corporation of the City of Washington receives *four hundred dollars* a year, *each,* for LICENSING PRIVATE SLAVE PRISONS. THE DISTRICT OF COLUMBIA IS ONE OF THE GREATEST AND MOST CRUEL SLAVE MARKETS IN THE WORLD !

Under the same authority FREE colored persons are thrown into prison, and if they cannot obtain evidence to prove their freedom, they are sold as slaves, *to pay jail fees ! Five persons have been sold, in one year, into perpetual slavery, to pay jail fees !*

The PUBLIC PRISONS of the United States, *maintained by taxes which we all pay,* are made use of by the slave dealers, to *store* the victims of the American slave trade.

The guilt of tolerating these enormities rests on the whole American people, and on every individual who will not exert himself to remove them. Congress, it is true, has the power of legislation. But it will never exercise the power, until the people require it. When the American people declare in a voice of thunder, that they will not endure to have their own metropolis profaned with Slavery, then, and not till then, will the legislation of Congress be the echo of their voice. Speak then, fellow citizens ! Overwhelm Congress with petitions, and tell your Representatives that Slavery and all traffic in human flesh at the Seat of Government must be TOTALLY, IMMEDIATELY, AND FOREVER ABOLISHED !

This broadside denounced the slave trade in the District of Columbia and encouraged abolitionists to send petitions to Congress. The slave trade was later abolished in Washington D.C. as a result of the Compromise of 1850.

what was needed to have his family released, and walked the rest of his way. Williams learned to his panic that he would need to raise $3,200 in one week. Fillmore promptly wrote a letter about Williams' need and gave the first contribution. With Fillmore's support and connections, Williams soon had enough to reclaim his family from their devastating fate.

Fillmore moved forward to put the controversial Compromise of 1850 into law. On August 6, he sent a strong message to Congress to settle the contentious issue. By September 18, Congress had separated the bill into separate sections and approved it. Fillmore, with the encouragement of his whole cabinet, then signed it into law. The night it was signed, the Union congressmen serenaded Fillmore at the White House. Fillmore bowed from a window at the mansion.

But outside of Washington, the Compromise did not sit as well. In the North, abolitionists abhorred the Compromise's tougher new version of the Fugitive Slave Law. Anyone who helped a fugitive slave in any way would be fined $1,000 and thrown into jail for six months, and if the slave got away, any person who had helped would have to pay $1,000 to the slave-owner to make up for his loss. Further, if a black person was brought to court and accused of being a fugitive slave, he could not speak on his own behalf. Not only that, but a judge who decided the accused was a fugitive slave would be paid ten dollars; deciding the accused was a free man or woman would only earn the judge five dollars. Once it was decided that the accused was a slave, U.S. marshals would return the person to his owner. Folks in the North claimed this meant that slave-catchers coming North could seize any blacks as runaways, even though they might have been free for years, and carry them back to slavery.

But the Compromise had also abolished the slave trade in Washington, D.C. and admitted California to the nation as a free, not a slave, state. The measure had also temporarily soothed sectional division. Fillmore wrote:

> The Compromise measures were not in all respects what I could have desired, but they were the best that could be obtained, after a protracted discussion that shook the Republic to its very foundation, and I felt bound to give them my official approval.[5]

"God knows that I detest slavery," Fillmore continued,

> but it is an existing evil, for which we are not responsible, and we must endure it, and give it such protection as is guaranteed by the Constitution, till we can get rid of it without destroying the last hope of free government in the world.[6]

It was with joy that Millard ordered the razing of the obnoxious slave pens that scarred the center of Washington, D.C. But when abolitionist mobs in Pennsylvania, New York, and Boston attacked federal marshals who were jailing fugitive slaves, Millard sent soldiers to enforce the law. It was, after all, the law of the land.

Near the end of his term, Fillmore pardoned two "slave-stealers" who had stolen seventy-seven Washington, D.C. slaves to help them find freedom in 1848. Their imprisonment for four years was very upsetting to all and Fillmore not only freed them, he gave them safe carriage rides out of the city for fear that slave-owners would have harmed them.

Once the agony of the Compromise of 1850 was over,

SOURCE DOCUMENT

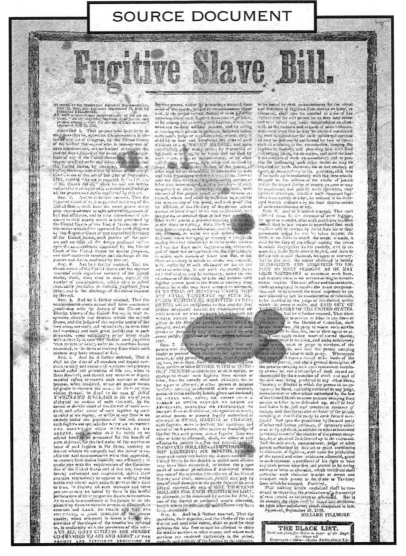

The Fugitive Slave Bill, approved by President Fillmore and passed as part of the Compromise of 1850 on September 18, 1850. Although Fillmore was personally opposed to slavery, he approved the Compromise of 1850, which included this fugitive slave law, in order to help soothe the sectional divisions within the nation.

President Fillmore dedicated the remainder of his term to helping the United States develop its economy. In December of 1850 Fillmore announced that negotiations had succeeded between the United States and England to mutually build and protect a ship canal between the Atlantic and Pacific Oceans somewhere in Central America. Many Forty-niners were already using a route across Panama by mule or foot. That year New York businessmen began a railroad across the very route that was to become the Panama Canal.

In May of 1851, Fillmore happily left Washington to celebrate the completion of the New York and Erie Railroad from New York City to Dunkirk, New York, on Lake Erie. This was the longest trunk line in the world at the time and the first railroad link between the Atlantic Seaboard and the Great Lakes. Governors, senators, congressmen, and cabinet members came along for the famous first ride.

The next month Fillmore ventured south, sailing down the Chesapeake Bay. When he was at the Richmond, Virginia, depot waiting to return to Washington, an old black slave stepped out of the crowd and tried to reach the platform. He held out his hand to shake the president's hand. A Richmond constable loudly sent him back, but when Fillmore noticed the commotion, he extended his arm and asked the black man to come forward. He grasped his hand warmly and said, "My old friend, I am glad to see you."[7] Tears ran down the humble man's face and soon Millard was gone.

On July 4, 1851, Millard laid the cornerstone for the extension of the Capitol. This was to add two massive wings, one to accommodate the Senate, and another for the House of Representatives. The capitol's large dome was also added at this time. Fillmore had not been happy with any of the architects' proposals, so he combined the best of several proposals to make sure that the harmony and beauty of the earlier building was not marred.

During his term President Fillmore also showed concern for social issues, especially at the urging of his friend Dorothea Dix, a champion of the mentally ill. She wanted decent asylums provided for the mentally ill, rather than degrading cages and cellars. Fillmore helped her procure funding from Congress and wrote her in congratulations. At President Fillmore's request, Congress also approved the building of a home to care for sick and poor veterans.[8]

In 1851, Millard accepted the vice presidency of a new organization called the American Colonization Society. The group wanted to end slavery by buying slaves from their owners, freeing them, and taking them to the west coast of Africa to live in a new black republic called Liberia. Gold washings had been found in the rivers of Africa and some thought it might be another California. Fillmore thought this was a productive way to calm the slave-owners, free the slaves, and save the nation from the future problem of integrating freed blacks into society.[9] Yet Fillmore's cabinet convinced him not to mention these plans in his annual message to Congress. Colonization would have cost $3 million dollars and was too volatile an idea for the time.

Even naming a governor for the Utah Territory was controversial. Mormons, led by Brigham Young, had settled in Salt Lake City. They had been expelled from several areas in the East because of their controversial belief in polygamy, in which a man takes multiple wives.

Fillmore, the only president of the times who was not prejudiced against the Mormons, logically named Young to be the first governor of the Utah Territory. In his honor, Millard County was formed and the town of Fillmore was temporarily named to be the site of Utah's new capital.

On Christmas Eve 1851, a tragic fire destroyed most of the Library of Congress—35,000 of the 55,000 books stored there. Fortunately the original draft of the Declaration of Independence was saved, as was most of the library of Thomas Jefferson. Fillmore left the White House and was right there with the firemen working at the engines to extinguish the blaze. He and his cabinet formed a bucket brigade and worked long hours into the night.[10]

Another sticky situation President Fillmore faced was how to handle General Kossuth, the intended liberator of Hungary from the power of Austria. Congress voted to send a battleship to Turkey to free this revolutionary from jail, and he later made his way to Washington to convince the American government to send soldiers to liberate Hungary. Fillmore told the general he sympathized with his struggle for freedom, but he made it clear that the United States would not interfere in European affairs. Kossuth was enraged and, with Seward's help, he used his great talent for speeches to condemn Fillmore for ignoring the "European" cause. In so doing, he and Seward gathered a lot of opposition to Fillmore among immigrant voters.[11]

Fillmore had problems in the Pacific to solve too. Several shipwrecked American sailors had washed up on Japanese shores, where they were treated poorly. The president decided to negotiate with Japan to protect the

U.S. sailors and to open Japanese ports to commercial trade with the United States. In November of 1852, Fillmore sent Admiral Matthew Perry to Japan, armed with full negotiation powers. The fleet, which did not arrive until July 1853, enjoyed a successful visit and signed a treaty with Japan, allowing the United States access to two small ports. This was the end of Japanese isolation and the beginning of Japan as a modern country.

Perry was not the only explorer sent out by Fillmore. He sent Lieutenant Lynch into Africa, Captain Ringgold into the Chinese seas, and Lieutenants Herndon and Gibbon into the Amazon region. In other foreign affairs, Fillmore negotiated for Peruvian guano, or seagull droppings, to be imported as fertilizer for American farms. He made a treaty between the United States and the king of the Hawaiian Islands, pledging to protect Hawaiian independence and prevent Louis Napoleon from annexing Hawaii for France. He also made Switzerland change prejudicial anti-Jewish language in a treaty of commerce and navigation.

During the 1850s some Southerners, hoping to find new potential slave regions, attempted to take over the island of Cuba from Spain. When Cuba captured and executed several of the extremists, Millard refused to retaliate against the mother country of Spain. He had warned the extremists that this was forbidden territory.

In the fall of 1850 Fillmore's family joined him in the White House. Abigail was reluctant to move in since Millard had written that it was "a temple of inconveniences."[12] She was also still mourning the death of her beloved sister.

Fillmore tried to improve conditions before his wife's

arrival. He asked the White House cook to modernize his kitchen with a new-fangled wood-stove. For years the old black cook had been preparing huge state dinners over an open hearth with pot-hooks, kettles, skillets, and cranes. The cook saw no reason to change, so Millard went to the Patent Office to learn how to use the new hotel-size cooking stove he had bought. Ever the teacher, he then taught the new methods of managing the drafts to the reluctant old cook.[13]

When Abigail arrived at the White House, she was amazed that eleven presidents had lived there before and still there was no library—no books, not even a Bible. She was used to ready access to her reference books, maps, and their own fully furnished library. Fillmore agreed it was unacceptable. In cabinet meetings, men had to scurry between offices to hunt for a law book or a dictionary.

On September 14, 1850, Abigail began a successful campaign to finance a library for the White House. She planned to entertain the most powerful congressmen for a series of Thursday night dinners until they agreed with her vision. Finally by March 3, 1851, the new congress permitted Abigail to spend two hundred fifty dollars "for the purchase of books for the library at the Executive Mansion . . . under the direction of the President of the U.S."[14]

Abigail set aside the largest, most cheerful room on the second floor for the library. It was here that the Fillmores invited their closest personal friends for happy musicals and informal visits. Even conscientious President Fillmore usually succeeded in leaving his Executive Chamber by 10:30 at night to spend a pleasant hour in the library with his family.[15] The public was interested in the First Lady's project. Visitors proclaimed the new library addition the White House's most comfortable and cheerful room.

Though Abigail officiated at weekly White House dinners, the Friday night receptions were very hard on her. She was expected to stand in the receiving line from eight to ten and her bad ankle made that very painful. She would sometimes stay in bed all day to rest up for the Friday night functions, but finally she gave the job over to young Abby, who had given up her teaching job in Buffalo to help her mother. Young Abby became the talk of Washington. She was self-possessed and had a rare ability to adapt her conversations to a variety of guests.

In January 1852, Abby's suitor Hiram Day visited Washington and stayed until March. The young couple accompanied Powers and his date to several balls, and the foursome traveled in the elegant family carriage.

Fillmore became the first president to be visited in the White House by his father, Nathaniel. Millard held a state banquet for him and introduced him to all the dignitaries and ambassadors of the time. Father and son stood side by side, with Nate still tall and erect at eighty. He was calm and poised in meeting all the judges and senators. One guest said, "You have been so successful in raising sons. I wish you would tell me how to bring up my little boy."

"Cradle him in a sap trough," said Nate, always ready with an answer.[16]

Powers served as his father's private secretary, and it was his task to arrange all the details of White House dinners, as well as small Saturday dinners, Tuesday luncheons, and entertainments. Band music was the usual fare.

First Lady Abigail Fillmore organized a White House library with funds solicited from Congress.

A typical White House dinner began with soup and fish, then offered a choice of nine entrees. Dinners ended with as many as four desserts, followed with fruits, coffee, and liqueurs, all served by six white-gloved waiters.[17]

The socialites of Washington were impressed with the handsome and intellectual First Lady Abigail Fillmore. She was the first wife of a president to have ever worked for a living, let alone earn an income after being married or becoming a mother. She was still an attractive woman at age fifty-two, with blue eyes and light brown curling hair. Abigail was also one of the first First Ladies to travel about Washington freely, gathering the cultural experiences that were like magnets to her. Accompanied by her daughter Abby, the very modern Mrs. Fillmore went to lectures, banquets, exhibitions of art, and literary meetings.

The Fillmores had always honored the Sabbath as a day for rest and meditation. When Fillmore became president, he found that Sundays had often been used by visitors for private interviews with the president. He put an end to that practice by ordering the doorkeeper to refuse all visitors, with no exceptions, and the family enjoyed one day of privacy and peace on Sundays in the closed White House.

Fillmore had enjoyed his first term in the White House, and though he did not seek a nomination for a second term, he was willing to go along with it if it was what his party wanted.

CHAPTER NINE

DOUBLE TRAGEDY

A t the 1852 Whig Convention held in Baltimore, Fillmore was, at first, the front-runner to be the Whig nominee for president. Many of his friends felt he was the only Whig with a chance to win. General Winfield Scott was right behind Fillmore in the ballots, and old Daniel Webster was way behind. Finally, after fifty-three votes, William Seward and Thurlow Weed convinced the people who were voting for Webster to put their votes on Scott, who then became the Whig candidate.

The Democrats, meanwhile, nominated Franklin Pierce of New Hampshire. Pierce's name had not come up at the Democratic convention until the thirty-third ballot, and Pierce won the nomination on the forty-ninth vote. It was a pretty dull campaign, and ironically, both parties endorsed the Compromise of 1850—the political burden

Democratic candidate Franklin Pierce replaced sitting President Millard Fillmore in the election of 1852.

that had allegedly kept Fillmore from being the candidate. Scott lost badly to Pierce, who never even left Concord, New Hampshire, during the whole political campaign.

In March 1853, when Fillmore left office, the nation was prosperous and contented, relations with foreign countries were smooth, and the cloud that had hung over the nation was seemingly gone.

On March 4, 1853, the liberated Mrs. Fillmore became the first First Lady to attend the inaugural of the man replacing her husband. On that raw and snowy day, she shivered as she stood with her literary friends, James Thackeray and Washington Irving, in an open stand.

Despite catching a cold, Abigail packed up all their personal possessions and enjoyed one last Washington shopping trip with Abby. She and Fillmore had made plans to build a new house in Buffalo and to tour the South on their way home. Neither had been south of Richmond and it would be a great adventure. Then she would happily return to a quiet private life.

But Abigail quickly became very ill. She was so congested that she could only sleep by resting her head on a table. A worried Fillmore wrote to his sister Julia after the first week of illness, reporting that Abigail spoke very little. He wrote to the new President Pierce that Mrs. Fillmore was indeed very sick.

On the 30th of March, fifty-five year-old Abigail died of pneumonia at the Willard Hotel near the White House. Fillmore was devastated. She had been his rock, his inspiration. "For twenty seven years," he wrote, "my entire married life, I was always greeted with a happy smile."[1] He had carefully preserved every line she ever wrote to him.

When Fillmore dejectedly settled back into his old home in Buffalo, he said: "But it does not seem like home. The light of the house is gone; and I can never hope to enjoy life again as I have heretofore."[2] He did not think it was right to practice law again as a former president—but what else was he to do?

Son Powers resumed his law practice, and Abby took over the running of the Fillmore household with grace and charm, system and regularity.

That Thanksgiving, Abby filled the house with Grandpa Nate and her Great Uncle Calvin and Great Aunt Julia. On New Years Eve, Fillmore spent a quiet night alone with his father in East Aurora. That winter he spent his afternoons reading history or science books, despite increasing problems with his eyesight. He also bought a house for his father and stepmother in the middle of town in East Aurora.

Bored and restless, Millard replanned his tour of the South, now without his precious Abigail. He worried a bit about leaving his children behind. "They are all that is left me of the dear, departed one . . . I could not reasonably hope that they would always remain with me. . . But I still hope for their society yet a little longer."[3] Traveling with

---

SOURCE DOCUMENT

In this April 12, 1853 letter to his sister Julia, Fillmore wrote that since his wife Abigail's death, "My home is deserted. Its great attraction is gone, and every object of her care while living but reminds me that she has gone never to return."

his former secretary of the Navy, John Kennedy, Fillmore was greeted with great honors throughout his lengthy trip to the South.

But in July of 1854 a second unspeakable tragedy happened. Fillmore's daughter 22-year-old Abby contracted cholera and died suddenly while visiting her grandparents in East Aurora, New York. Fillmore and Powers were both sick with grief. Since her mother's death, Abby had given her whole mind and heart to caring for her brother and father, and they had repaid her devotion with the kindest and most grateful affection.

Fillmore wrote his friend Dorothea Dix, "My good son, only, of all my little family remains. I have none other now to sympathize with me in grief or rejoice with me in prosperity. And my dwelling, once so cheerful and happy, is now dark and desolate."[4]

Hiram Day, Abby's suitor, lived to be an old man and never married anyone else. His heart had belonged to Abby alone.

Almost immediately after Abby's funeral, Fillmore and Powers left their home to seek the comfort of old friends and relatives in Moravia, Skaneateles, Montville, and New Hope. Dorothea Dix wrote with a prescription for Millard's depression—a trip to Europe to "occupy the winter in seeing what is most worthy of study and observation in the old civilized world."[5]

In May of 1855 Fillmore took Dix's advice. He sailed to Liverpool on the steamer *Atlantic* to seek distraction among the art and treasures of Europe. Over there he could also ignore the growing tension in the nation. The Kansas-Nebraska Act, passed in 1854, had allowed settlers in the territories to decide for themselves whether their region would be slave or free. This had led to violence between proslavery and antislavery settlers in the Kansas Territory, including an incident in which abolitionist John Brown and his followers murdered five proslavery men. The violence had spilled over into the Senate, where Massachusetts Senator Charles Sumner, an avid abolitionist, delivered a speech denouncing what he called "The Crime against Kansas." Two days later, Congressman Preston Brooks of South Carolina savagely beat Sumner over the head with a heavy cane until the cane snapped and the bleeding senator was unconscious. Sumner was in bed for two years and never fully recovered from the attack.[6]

President Pierce, who had come out for slavery in his inaugural speech, had promptly created chaos by replacing the thirty-year-old Missouri Compromise with a plan to make slavery legal in a huge new area, all the way up to the Canadian border. The dormant quarrel over the expansion of slavery that had been sleeping since the Compromise of 1850 was fully awake again. It was a good time to get away.

In England Fillmore and Martin Van Buren, the first two former presidents to visit England, appeared together in the gallery of the House of Commons. Millard even visited Westminster Abbey, where he was presented to Queen Victoria at the Court of St. James. Fillmore's travel companion, General James Wilson, wrote that Fillmore was dressed

> in complete court costume—cocked hat, sword, knee breeches, silk stockings, and silver buckled shoes—all which set off his fine face and figure to the greatest advantage. Taking a passing survey of himself in the large mirror . . . he said with a merry laugh . . . "Well, gentleman, I never expected to come to this.[7]

Oxford University offered to bestow Fillmore with a Degree of Classical Languages, but Millard humbly declined, feeling the honor was offered more because he was a former president than for his own intellect. "I had not the advantage of a classical education, and no man should in my opinion accept a degree that he cannot read."[8]

Joining up with Kennedy again and William Corcoran, Millard traveled to Paris to view the International Exposition. There they were presented to Emperor Napoleon III. In August they visited Brussels and Cologne, then boated up the Rhine to Geneva, Switzerland. There was hardly a city missed—Munich, Vienna, Prague, Dresden, Berlin, Hamburg, Hanover, Bremen, Dusseldorf, Amsterdam, Antwerp, and back to Paris.[9]

In Paris in November, he joined Buffalo publisher Dr. Thomas Foote and Elam Jewett. They toured the Riviera on their way to Italy, arriving in Rome near Christmas.

Here Fillmore faced a political dilemma. He was offered a private audience with Pope Pius IX, the head of the Catholic Church since 1846. But in 1854 Fillmore had made the decision to join the American Party, which was in many ways the opposite of the Anti-Masonic Party with which he had begun his political career. To join the American Party, also known as the Know-Nothing Party, one had to follow an elaborate secret ritual and unite with the Order of the Star-Spangled Banner, an anti-Catholic secret society. Even the initiation questions were written in a secret code. When members were asked details about the party, they were told to say, "I know nothing," hence its nickname—the Know-Nothing Party. Only native-born, white Americans with no Catholic connections were eligible.[10]

The members of the American Party feared the huge influx of immigrants, who were now arriving at a rate three times faster than ever before in the nineteenth century.

SOURCE DOCUMENT

PLATFORM OF THE AMERICAN PARTY.

I. An humble acknowledgment to the Supreme Being who rules the universe, for His protecting care vouchsafed to our fathers in their revolutionary struggle, and hitherto manifested to us, their descendants, in the preservation of the liberties, the independence and the union of these states.

II. The perpetuation of the Federal Union, as the palladium of our civil and religious liberties, and the only sure bulwark of American independence.

III. *Americans must rule America*, and to this end, *native*-born citizens should be selected for all state, federal or municipal offices or government employment, in preference to naturalized citizens—*nevertheless,*

IV. Persons born of American parents residing temporarily abroad, shall be entitled to all the rights of native-born citizens; but

V. No person should be selected for political station (whether of native or foreign birth), who recognises any alliance or obligation of any description to any foreign prince, potentate or power, who refuses to recognise the federal and state constitutions (each within its sphere), as paramount to all other laws, as rules of particular action.

VI. The unqualified recognition and maintenance of the reserved rights of the several states, and the cultivation of harmony and fraternal good-will between the citizens of the several states, and to this end, non-interference by Congress with questions appertaining solely to the individual states, and non-intervention by each state with the affairs of any other state.

VII. The recognition of the right of the native-born and naturalized citizens of the United States, permanently residing in any territory thereof, to frame their constitution and laws, and to regulate their domestic and social affairs in their own mode, subject only to the provisions of the Federal Constitution, with the right of admission into the Union whenever they have the requisite population for one representative in Congress. *Provided always,* that none but those who are citizens of the United States, under the Constitution and laws thereof, and who have fixed residence in any such territory, ought to participate in the formation of the constitution, or in the enactment of laws for said territory or state.

VIII. An enforcement of the principle that no state or territory can admit others than native-born citizens to the right of suffrage, or of holding political office, unless such persons shall have been naturalized according to the laws of the United States.

IX. A change in the laws of naturalization, making a continued residence of twenty-one years, of all not heretofore provided for, an indispensable requisite for citizenship hereafter, and excluding all paupers and persons convicted of crime from landing on our shores; but no interference with the vested rights of foreigners.

The American Party, also known as the Know-Nothing Party, sought to restrict voting and office holding to native-born citizens. The party garnered support from those who feared immigrants were threatening American democratic institutions and ways of life.

The Know-Nothings wanted to make it impossible for these "invaders" to hold public office in the United States.

While Fillmore believed many immigrants were hard working, good people, he and other American Party members were concerned that the huge volume of new immigrants also included those who had nothing in common with U.S. citizens and who did not appreciate American values. Fillmore said,

> Our immigrants are no longer mainly Protestants. A majority of them no longer come from the country whose language we speak, by whose literature our minds are formed, from whom we have borrowed the habeas corpus, trial by jury, representative government, and the common law. We receive now, with a great many estimable, industrious, self-respecting people, the very dregs and scum of the population of Europe. All that is benighted by ignorance . . . all that is detestable in morals, all that is odious and abominable by crime have, for the last few years, been poured upon our shores, to taint our moral atmosphere, and add to the corruption of our large cities.[11]

When Fillmore was told he would be expected to kneel and kiss the hand and maybe the foot of the Pope, he canceled the meeting. Finally, an embassy official assured him that this was not the case, and Fillmore decided to meet with the Pope after all. The Pope received him, "offering neither hand nor foot for salutation, and to my surprise asked me to take a seat. He has a very benevolent face and I doubt not is a very good man."[12]

On February 22, 1856, while in Rome, Fillmore received a letter telling him that had been nominated as the American Party's presidential candidate. His running mate would be Andrew Jackson Donelson. Friends wrote

SOURCE DOCUMENT

MILLARD FILLMORE,

AMERICAN CANDIDATE FOR PRESIDENT OF THE UNITED STATES.

An 1856 campaign poster showing American Party candidate Millard Fillmore.

to Fillmore, urging him to run again. In May, Fillmore wrote back that he would accept the nomination and run for the presidency.

Fillmore may have accepted the American Party's nomination because he believed he was the only one who could keep the country together. The Republican Party was too tied with the abolitionists, the Democrats were proslavery, and the Whig Party had disintegrated. Fillmore disliked the new Republicans, predicting accurately that if this extremist group ever elected a president, the South would secede.

Fillmore had seen the negative impact the flood of

immigrants had on the nation's cities, with dangerous slums, crime, and mob violence. He knew that slimy politicians were rounding up new immigrants and buying their votes with food, drink, and promises of jobs. Now that he had seen first-hand the sad conditions of some Europeans, he did not want to deny them the opportunity to come to America for a new life. But he wanted to preserve American traditions of democracy and worried about the newcomers' ability to subscribe to American democratic values.

Fillmore soon returned to the United States, arriving in New York Harbor on June 22, 1856. The ship he was on fired its gun and rockets until it was docked. The wharf answered with a fifty-gun salute from the New Jersey shore. Over two thousand people waited to greet the presidential candidate, giving hearty cheers for Millard Fillmore. They paraded up Canal to Broadway. From almost every window, ladies waved white handkerchiefs in greeting.

On the whistle-stop train ride home, Fillmore stopped to cheering crowds in city after city, spreading the message that Americans should govern Americans. Fillmore said, "I regret to say that men who come fresh from the monarchies of the Old World are prepared neither by education, habits of thought, or knowledge of our institutions to govern Americans."[13]

Main Street in Buffalo, New York, had been decorated with flags and buntings and as the carriages of the parade passed by, bouquets of flowers were thrown down from the women who filled the office windows.[14] When Fillmore at last closed the door of his home on Franklin Street, a band outside played "Home, Sweet Home."[15]

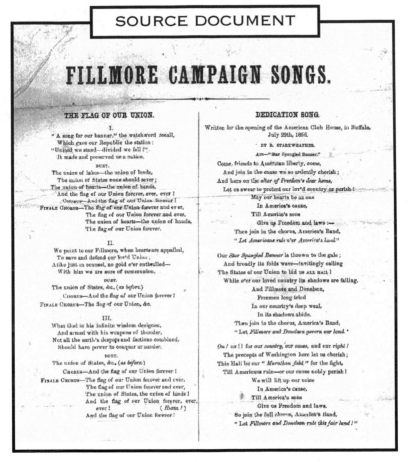

These songs were written to promote Fillmore's 1856 campaign as the American Party candidate for president.

Fillmore began his campaign by writing letters expressing his opinions to friends in other cities, knowing that these would be published in each city's newspapers. Since Donelson, his running partner, was from the South, their motto was "Fillmore and Our Whole Country!"

In contrast, both the Democrats and Republicans were running only northern candidates.

Fillmore wanted to unite the nation and he resolved to "look upon this whole country, from the farthest coast of Maine to the utmost limit of Texas, as but one country."[16]

> If there be those, North or South, who desire an administration for the North as against the South, or for the South as against the North, they are not the men who should give their suffrages to me. For my own part, I know only my whole country, and nothing but my country.[17]

Others felt that Fillmore was the one man who could heal the divided nation.

Edward Bates, a former Whig and later Lincoln's attorney general, said, "Nothing but Fillmore's election" could fix the state of the national divisions. "And my prayer to God is that He will bless the nation by enabling us to place at its head a man of moderation, order and peace."[18]

"We are treading upon the brink of a volcano," Fillmore warned the nation. "You must see that if this sectional fabric succeeds, it leads inevitably to the destruction of this beautiful fabric reared by our forefathers, cemented by their blood, and bequeathed to us as a priceless inheritance."[19] Fillmore warned that if the Union were dissolved, it would not be divided into two republics or two monarchies, but broken into fragments at war with each other.

The Republicans had chosen John Frémont as their candidate. He was famous as a pathfinder, having made exploratory trips to the West with Kit Carson. The Democrats ran James Buchanan, whose advantage was that he had been in London during the discussion of the Kansas-Nebraska Act and had not taken a stand on it.

In November of 1856 the votes were cast and Fillmore lost to the Democratic candidate, James Buchanan, coming in third with only 22 percent of the popular vote compared to Buchanan's 45 percent and Frémont's 33 percent.[20]

It was time for Fillmore to say goodbye to politics forever. He had had enough.

CHAPTER TEN

A NEW LIFE

In 1857 Fillmore met Caroline Carmichael McIntosh, an intelligent, cultured, and very wealthy widow. Her first husband, widower Ezekiel McIntosh, had made a fortune in crockery and in building the railroad between Albany and Schenectady, but had died suddenly after a tour of Europe in 1855.[1]

Widow Caroline McIntosh lived in the imposing Schuyler Mansion, high on a bluff overlooking Albany. She posed a contrast to the simple style of Abigail. Short and plump, she decked herself with fabulous jewels and elegant clothes.[2] But despite her many differences from his beloved Abigail, Fillmore was indeed very interested.

Fillmore still cut a dashing figure. His usual attire was a glossy black coat, a stiffly starched high-collared shirt, a black silk bow tie, and white kid gloves. His kindly blue eyes and gracious manner charmed Mrs. McIntosh.

Fillmore and his second wife, Caroline Carmichael McIntosh, moved into this mansion off Niagara Square in Buffalo, New York.

The financial Panic of 1857 gave Fillmore more reason to marry. Many of his investments suffered badly, and he was no longer practicing law to provide an income. His son Powers was against the marriage, and Caroline was not so sure either, wanting to stay in her Albany mansion. But finally she consented, and the delicate negotiations began.

Caroline agreed she would rent her home, and they bought the fourteen-room Hollister Mansion on Niagara Square, the most enormous house in town. The couple signed a pre-nuptial agreement, allowing Caroline to keep all her property in her name, although Fillmore was allowed to manage it. He could not, however, sell anything of Caroline's without her permission. He would earn ten thousand dollars a year for being his wife's financial manager.

The front hall inside the main entrance of Fillmore's Niagara Square home in Buffalo.

The couple was married on February 11, 1858, in Albany. Caroline was forty-five, thirteen years younger than her new husband. The Fillmores took a winter-long honeymoon in Europe, where Caroline collected many items to fill her home in the elegant Victorian fashion. She had a passion for pictures and lined every wall with pictures of herself and Millard, as well as the rest of the family.[3] She also ordered the addition of two towers in the front of the mansion, earning the house the nickname of "The Castle."

Gradually the new Fillmore couple settled into their new married life. Caroline religiously kept scrapbooks of newspaper clippings on all kinds of topics, but especially her husband's life. She also painted landscapes. Fillmore's joy was still reading. Anyone passing by could count on seeing him sitting at the deep front window, reading the morning papers. He also enjoyed history, philosophy, and occasionally a novel or book of poetry.[4] His extensive book collection now contained over five thousand volumes, housed in two libraries in the upper and middle halls and his office. The books were well-organized and carefully catalogued—including sixty-seven dictionaries and twenty-one grammar books.

For their daily outings the Fillmores rode in their black coupe for about two miles, then Millard would climb out and walk back. The carriage was ordered to keep pace with his walk so that both arrived home at the same time.[5]

Fillmore avoided politics now, even though he had strong opinions. After the attack by the abolitionist John Brown and his followers on the federal arsenal at Harpers Ferry in October of 1859, he blamed his successor, Democrat Franklin Pierce, for the inept Kansas-Nebraska Act, saying, "The lamentable tragedy at Harpers Ferry is clearly traceable to this unfortunate controversy about slavery in Kansas."[6]

At the 1860 Republican convention, Abraham Lincoln received the Republican presidential nomination. He went on to win the election that year. Within days of Lincoln's election, the Union was broken. South Carolina seceded, followed by five more southern states before Lincoln's inauguration.

On Saturday, February 16, 1861, President-elect Abraham Lincoln came through Buffalo on his way to his inauguration. The next day, Caroline and Millard accompanied him to the First Unitarian Church. The men also appeared together on the balcony of the American Hotel to greet a huge crowd.

Two months later, after the Civil War between the North and South had begun, Millard Fillmore returned once again to stand in front of the American Hotel, this time calling for volunteers for the war effort. As chairman of the Buffalo Committee of Public Defense, Fillmore organized a huge Union rally to encourage the patriotic fervor of Buffalo's citizens. He organized retired militiamen too old to bear arms into Union Continentals, who escorted departing troops to the train station, provided honor guards at funerals, and marched in Fourth of July parades.

Since his defeat in 1856 Fillmore had shunned politics.[7] But he generously contributed to the Union Defense Committee to raise funds for the support of soldiers' families.

On Christmas Eve in 1861, Fillmore's dear friend and former law partner Solomon Haven died. Fillmore was too emotional to speak at his funeral.

Millard Fillmore's new mission in life became the betterment of his beloved city of Buffalo. He helped begin the Buffalo Fine Arts Academy, making Buffalo only the fourth city in the country to have a permanent art gallery. In May 1862, Fillmore was voted the first president of the Buffalo Historical Society. He presided over its meetings, which were held in the homes of members during the long snow-bound winters. At each meeting, they shared papers members had researched and written about various historical subjects.[8] When Fillmore was seventy-one, the group coaxed him to write the story of his life. He did, focusing completely on his early years, and he required that his autobiography stay sealed until after his death.

On March 28, 1863, Fillmore's father died at the age of ninety-one. Fillmore buried him beside his mother in the Pioneer Cemetery in East Aurora.

In 1864, Lincoln ran for re-election against Democrat General George McClellan, whom Fillmore supported. Fillmore opposed many of the Republican policies of Lincoln, calling them "national bankruptcy and military despotism" which led to sharp criticism of Fillmore, who was even accused of treason by some Republican newspapers.[9] He was deeply hurt by the accusations and withdrew even more from public life. Meanwhile, he was personally sickened by news of the bloody Civil War battles.

President Lincoln won re-election and shortly after his second inauguration, he was assassinated in April 1865. At the time, Fillmore's wife Caroline was having one of her sick spells, and the Fillmore home had not yet been draped with the black buntings that people used then to mourn important public figures such as President Lincoln. An angry mob, thinking it was a political statement by the ex-president, came to Fillmore's home and smeared the Castle with ink. Fillmore emerged from the mansion and pleaded ignorance of Lincoln's death because of tending to his wife's needs. He quickly ordered the draping to be put up, but still felt a pang of sadness and fear when he spotted a crude hanging dummy in the square, an effigy of himself placed there by the angry mob.[10]

Twelve days after Lincoln's death, Fillmore redeemed himself by leading the Union Continentals in escorting the funeral train on its way to Lincoln's final resting place

SOURCE DOCUMENT

Buffalo, Feby. 20. 1873,

Hon. L. Bradford Prince
Chairman &c
Sir
I understand that a bill which has passed the senate, to amend the law to prevent cruelty to animals, is now before the committee over which you preside, and although I have not seen the bill in its amended form, yet from the information which I have of its contents, I beg leave most respectfully but earnestly to urge its passage.

Respectfully yours
Millard Fillmore

Among his many civic activities, Fillmore helped found a Buffalo Society for the Prevention of Cruelty to Animals. In this 1873 letter he urged the passage of a bill to prevent cruelty to animals.

in Springfield, Illinois. The funeral train traveled Lincoln's inauguration route in reverse and in quite the opposite mood. Everywhere Americans displayed their grief, with evergreens, flowers, and buntings. In Buffalo over one hundred thousand came to weep over the blossom-strewn open casket until the doors were closed at 8 P.M.

After the Civil War ended, life in Buffalo settled back to normal. At the Castle, Millard and Caroline entertained visitors such as Prince Arthur of England, a Japanese ambassador, and President Andrew Johnson in 1866. Caroline enjoyed taking guests around to admire the busts and paintings of her eminent husband. And everyone noticed the sweet courtesies that Millard paid to his wife Caroline, such as kneeling to adjust her overshoes before she climbed into their carriage.

The next year, Fillmore made what was to be his last trip to Europe with Caroline. And back in Buffalo, Fillmore had a part in seemingly every cultural group. He helped to found and served as the first president of the Buffalo Club, an exclusive male group of wealthy lawyers, prominent judges, bankers, and heads of industry and business in Buffalo. Fillmore also helped begin Buffalo General Hospital, the Grosvenor Library, the Society for the Prevention of Cruelty to Animals, and the Buffalo Museum of Science.

In 1873 a reunion of the last five Fillmore siblings was held at Millard's brother Calvin's home in Michigan. Olive Johnson was seventy-five, a widow; Cyrus was seventy-one; Calvin sixty-three; Millard seventy-three; and Julia Harris, also a widow, was sixty-one. A photo was taken to celebrate their longevity.[11]

The next year, Fillmore felt his left hand paralyze

Former President Fillmore died on March 8, 1874 at age seventy-four.

while he was shaving. The paralysis extended to the left side of his face. Two weeks later, he had another stroke. On March 2, he received the devastating news that his life-long friend Nathan Hall had died. Finally on March 8, 1874, at 11:10 P.M., Fillmore died in his library.

Fillmore's funeral, held March 11, was attended by President Ulysses S. Grant and many other dignitaries. Fillmore was buried in Forest Lawn Cemetery, at last rejoining his beloved Abigail and Abby. Not far away lay the other members of the old firm of Fillmore, Hall, & Haven, ironically even in the proper order.[12] The tributes flowed. General James Wilson said, "The president's dream was peace. If by indulging in this delusive death, he erred, it surely was an error that leaned in virtue's side."[13]

Fillmore stood as a testament to the American dream, working hard for all that he had accomplished. He was willing to sacrifice his good name and political future in order to keep his beloved country together. If President Taylor had not died, putting the moderate and courageous Fillmore at the helm of the country, the Civil War could easily have begun a decade sooner. The eleven years that Fillmore's pursuit of compromise bought for the country allowed the North to develop its industry and railroad network, both of which were advantages that later helped the North win the war. In delaying the Civil War, perhaps it is Fillmore to whom we owe our gratitude that today we are one country.

CHRONOLOGY

1800   Born on January 7 in Cayuga County, New York.

1814   Apprenticed to learn wool carding in Sparta, New York.

1819   Began study of law under Quaker Judge Wood of Moravia, New York.

1823   Admitted to practice at Court of Common Pleas in Buffalo.

1826   Married Abigail Powers.

1827   Became attorney of the state supreme court.

1828   Birth of son, Powers. Elected to New York state assembly as the Anti-Masonic Party candidate.

1829   Re-elected to state assembly.

1830   Re-elected to state assembly.

1831   Drafted and led adoption of a bill abolishing debtors' prison.

1832   Formed law firm of Clary & Fillmore. Birth of daughter, Mary Abigail. Elected U.S. Representative to Congress.

1834   Formed law firm of Fillmore & Hall.

1836   Formed law firm of Fillmore, Hall & Haven. Re-elected U.S. Representative to Congress.

1838   Re-elected U.S. Representative to Congress.

1840   Re-elected U.S. Representative to Congress, chaired Ways & Means Committee.

1842   Sponsored support of Samuel Morse's telegraph. Declined nomination to Congress.

1844   Was candidate for vice president at the Whig convention in Baltimore. Nominated for governor of New York, defeated by Silas Wright

1846
–1874 Chancellor of the University of Buffalo.

1847 Elected first comptroller of New York.

1848 Nominated for vice president by the Whig Party. Elected vice president with Zachary Taylor as president.

1849 Inaugurated as vice president of the United States.

1850 Taylor dies; Fillmore takes oath of office as president of the United States. Approved the Compromise of 1850.

1852 Sent Admiral Perry to Japan.

1853 Retired from the presidency. Abigail died in Washington, D.C.

1854 Daughter Abby died.

1856 Nominated for president by the American Party; defeated in the election.

1858 Married Mrs. Caroline C. McIntosh.

1862 Chairman, Buffalo Committee of Public Defense. Chosen first president of Buffalo Historical Society, serves until 1867

1867 First president of Buffalo Club.

1870 President of Buffalo General Hospital.

1870
–1874 Trustee of Grosvenor Library, Buffalo.

1874 Died on March 8th at his home in Buffalo.

DID YOU KNOW?

Trivia from the President's Lifetime

Did you know that ready-made apparel first appeared in shops in the United States in the 1820s? Among the first to sell mass-produced clothing was Henry Sands Brooks of New York City, whose store is known today as Brooks Brothers. Before this time most clothing was made by women at home, or by tailors who cus-tom-made clothing for their clients.

Did you know that Cyrus McCormick, the son of a farmer, patented an invention called the mechanical reaper in 1834? This horse-drawn machine positioned grain stalks and then cut and felled them onto a platform. McCormick's mechanical reaper reduced the number of people needed to harvest grain and sped up the process, allowing farmers to plant far more wheat than ever before.

Did you know that birthrates declined in the United States during the nineteenth century? For economic and social reasons, Americans began to see small families as more desirable. In 1800 an American woman gave birth to an average of six to seven chil-dren. By 1860, that number had declined to five, and by 1900, four.

Did you know that 3.3 million immigrants entered the United States between 1847 and 1857? Revolutions, civil unrest, and famine in Europe sent a wave of immigrants to the United States during this period. Most immigrants flocked to cities in search of work, altering the ethnic makeup of the nation's urban areas. In 1845, 35 percent of New York City residents were foreign born; by 1855, 52 percent of the city's population had been born in another country.

CHAPTER NOTES

Chapter One: A Nation in Turmoil
1. Benson Lee Grayson, *The Unknown President: The Administration of President Millard Fillmore* (University Press of America, Inc. 1981), p. 33.
2. Robert Rayback, *Millard Fillmore: Biography of a President* (Newtown, Connecticut: American Political Biography Press), p. 211.
3. Joseph Ellis, *Founding Brothers: The Revolutionary Generation* (New York: Alfred Knopf, 2001), p. 88.
4. Rayback, p. 219.
5. Rayback, p. 211.
6. Charles Snyder, *The Lady and the President: The Letters of Dorothea Dix and Millard Fillmore* (Louisville: University Press of Kentucky, 1975), p. 42;
7. Obituary of Millard Fillmore, *New York Times*.

Chapter Two: The Log Cabin
1. Letter of Nathaniel Fillmore to Rev. Hosmer, March 3, 1851, Buffalo and Erie County Historical Society; Proceedings of the Buffalo Historical Society, p. 510.
2. Rev. G. W. Hosmer, advance sheets of American Genealogical Register, January 1877
3. *Syracuse Herald*, July 17, 1935.
4. Millard Fillmore, *The Early Life of Millard Fillmore* (Buffalo: Salisbury Club, 1958)
5. Lucy Lord, 1/10/1899, quoting Millard Fillmore at Buffalo Society for the Protection of Animals, Proceedings of the Buffalo Historical Society, p. 517.
6. 1836 school directory of Summer Hill, Buffalo and Erie County Historical Society.
7. Millard Fillmore, *The Early Life of Millard Fillmore* (Buffalo: Salisbury Club, 1958).

Chapter Three: Handling the Rowdies
1. Millard Fillmore, *Millard Fillmore, The Early Life of Millard Fillmore* (Buffalo: Salisbury Club, 1958).
2. Ibid.
3. Ibid.
4. Ibid.

5. Frank Severance, "Letters Before the Civil War," Vol. X. Publications of the Buffalo Historical Society, p. 384.

6. *Caroline's Scrapbook*, Vol. 15, Buffalo and Erie County Historical Society.

7. Millard Fillmore, *The Early Life of Millard Fillmore* (Buffalo: Salisbury Club, 1958).

8. Frank H. Severance, *Millard Fillmore Papers*, Vol. 1, (Buffalo, New York: Buffalo Historical Society, 1907)

9. Millard Fillmore, *The Early Life of Millard Fillmore* (Buffalo: Salisbury Club, 1958).

10. Ibid.

Chapter Four: A Reason to Achieve

1. Millard Fillmore, *The Early Life of Millard Fillmore* (Buffalo: Salisbury Club, 1958).

2. Ibid.

3. Ibid.

4. *Caroline's Scrapbook*, Vol. 15, Buffalo and Erie County Historical Society.

5. Millard Fillmore, *The Early Life of Millard Fillmore* (Buffalo: Salisbury Club, 1958).

6. Letter qualifying Fillmore to teach school, Collection of Buffalo and Erie County Historical Society.

7. Millard Fillmore, *The Early Life of Millard Fillmore* (Buffalo: Salisbury Club, 1958).

8. Ibid.

9. Ibid.

10. Ibid.

11. *New York Times*, March 9, 1874.

12. Charles Snyder, *The Lady and the President: The Letters of Dorothea Dix and Millard Fillmore* (Louisville: University Press of Kentucky, 1975), p. 29.

Chapter Five: Entering Politics

1. Crisfield Johnson, *Centennial History of Erie County, New York* (Buffalo, House of Matthews and Warren, 1876), p. 388.

2. Aurora Union Debating Society records, Aurora Historical Society.

Chapter Six: Fillmore, Hall, and Haven

1. Hiram Day quoted in Frank H. Severance, *Millard Fillmore Papers*, Vol. II, (Buffalo, New York: Buffalo Historical Society, 1907), p. 506.

2. Samuel Welch, *Recollections of Buffalo During the Decade from 1830-1840, 1830-1840* (Buffalo, New York: P. Paul and Bros. 1891), p. 5.
3. Welch, pp. 380–381.
4. Mrs. Solomon Haven, "Recollections of President Fillmore," from Frank H. Severance, *Millard Fillmore Papers*, Vol. II, (Buffalo, New York: Buffalo Historical Society, 1907), p. 489.
5. Ibid.

Chapter Seven: Leader of the Whigs

1. John Robert Irelan, *History of the Life, Administration, and Times of Millard Fillmore: Thirteenth President of the United States* (Chicago: Fairbanks & Palmer Publishing Co.,1888), p. 163.
2. Frank Severance, "Letters Before the Civil War," Vol. X., Publications of the Buffalo Historical Society, p. 234.
3. Irelan, p. 59.
4. Samuel Morse telegraph message, <http://inventors.about.com/library/inventors/bltelegraph.htm> (May 15, 2003).
5. Lawrence, p. 302.
6. Robert Rayback, *Millard Fillmore: Biography of a President* (Newtown, Connecticut: American Political Biography Press), p. 160.
7. Obituary of Millard Powers Fillmore, *Buffalo Commercial Advertiser*, November 16, 1889.
8. Hiram Day, "Recollections of President Fillmore," in Frank H. Severance, *Millard Fillmore Papers*, Vol. XI, (Buffalo, New York: Buffalo Historical Society, 1907), p. 489.
9. Irelan, p. 82.
10. Hiram Day, "Recollections of President Fillmore," in Frank H. Severance, *Millard Fillmore Papers*, Vol. XI, p. 506.
11. Rayback, p. 172.
12. Rayback, pp. 148, 186.

Chapter Eight: The Thirteenth President

1. Mrs. Solomon Haven, "Recollections of President Fillmore," from Frank H. Severance, *Millard Fillmore Papers*, Vol. II, (Buffalo, New York: Buffalo Historical Society, 1907), p. 491.
2. *Caroline's Scrapbook*, Vol. 15, Buffalo and Erie County Historical Society.
3. Frank H. Severance, *Millard Fillmore Papers*, Vol. X., (Buffalo, New York: Buffalo Historical Society, 1907), p. 431.

4. Mark Stegmaier, "The Case of the Coachman's Family: An Incident of President Fillmore's Administration," *Civil War History*, Vol. XXXII, No. 4 (Kent, Ohio: Ohio State University Press, 1986).
5. Frank H. Severance, *Millard Fillmore Papers*, Vol. X, p. 432.
6. Frank H. Severance, *Millard Fillmore Papers*, Vol. X, p. 335.
7. *Caroline's Scrapbook*, Vol. 15.
8. Charles Snyder, *The Lady and the President: The Letters of Dorothea Dix and Millard Fillmore* (Louisville: University Press of Kentucky, 1975), p. 137.
9. Robert Rayback, *Millard Fillmore: Biography of a President* (Newtown, Connecticut: American Political Biography Press), p. 369.
10. Louise Payson Latimer, *Your Washington and Mine* (New York: Charles Scribner's Sons, 1924), p. 66.
11. Elbert B. Smith, *The Presidencies of Zachary Taylor and Millard Fillmore* (University Press of Kansas, 1988), pp. 231–233.
12. Frank H. Severance, *Millard Fillmore Papers*, Vol. XI, p. 306.
13. Bess Furman, *White House Profile: A Social History of the White House, Its Occupants, and Its Festivities* (Indianapolis: Bobbs-Merrill, 1951), p. 155.
14. Millard Fillmore letter to Congress, September 23, 1850.
15. Mrs. Solomon Haven "Recollections of President Fillmore" in Frank H. Severance, *Millard Fillmore Papers*, Vol. XI, p. 492.
16. Ibid.
17. Frank H. Severance, *Millard Fillmore Papers*, Vol. XI, pp. 515–516.

Chapter Nine: Double Tragedy

1. Millard Fillmore letter to Julia Harris, April 13, 1853, Buffalo and Erie County Historical Society.
2. Charles Snyder, *The Lady and the President: The Letters of Dorothea Dix and Millard Fillmore* (Louisville: University Press of Kentucky, 1975), p. 150.
3. Millard Fillmore letter to Julia Harris, April 13, 1853, Buffalo and Erie County Historical Society.
4. Millard Fillmore letter, August 29, 1854, Buffalo and Erie County Historical Society.
5. Snyder, p. 212.
6. Lawrence, p. 332–333.
7. Frank H. Severance, *Millard Fillmore Papers*, Vol. XI., (Buffalo, New York: Buffalo Historical Society, 1907), p. 470.
8. Ibid, p. 483.
9. Snyder, pp. 241–243.

10. Lawrence, p. 330.
11. *Caroline's Scrapbook*, Vol. 15, Buffalo and Erie County Historical Society.
12. Severance, *Millard Fillmore Papers*, Vol. XI, p. 356.
13. W.L. Barre, *The Life and Public Services of Millard Fillmore* (Buffalo, New York: Wanzer, McKim, and Co., 1856) p. 241.
14. Severance, *Millard Fillmore Papers*, Vol. XI, p. 31
15. Ibid.
16. Severance, *Millard Fillmore Papers*, Vol. X, p. 431.
17. Cover of "Fillmore Quick Step" campaign song sheet music, Aurora Historical Society, New York.
18. Edward Bates letter to Millard Fillmore, September 24, 1856.
19. John Robert Irelan, *History of the Life, Administration, and Times of Millard Fillmore: Thirteenth President of the United States* (Chicago: Fairbanks & Palmer Publishing Co.,1888), p. 424.
20. Mary Beth Norton, et al, *A People and a Nation*, Vol. 1 (Boston: Houghton-Mifflin Co., 1990), p. A-27.

Chapter 10: A New Life

1. Will of Ezekiel McIntosh.
2. *Caroline's Scrapbook*, Vol. 15, Buffalo and Erie County Historical Society; John Robert Irelan, History of the Life, Administration, and Times of Millard Fillmore: Thirteenth President of the United States (Chicago: Fairbanks & Palmer Publishing Co.,1888), p. 472.
3. Irelan, pp. 473–474.
4. *Caroline's Scrapbook*, Vol. 15.
5. Ibid.
6. Charles Snyder, *The Lady and the President: The Letters of Dorothea Dix and Millard Fillmore* (Louisville: University Press of Kentucky, 1975), pp. 325-326.
7. *Caroline's Scrapbook*, Vol. 15, Buffalo and Erie County Historical Society, New York.
8. Frank H. Severance, *Millard Fillmore Papers*, Vol. XI., (Buffalo, New York: Buffalo Historical Society, 1907), p. 515.
9. Robert Rayback, *Millard Fillmore: Biography of a President* (Newtown, Connecticut: American Political Biography Press), p. 429.
10. *Buffalo Express*, April 17 and 18, 1865.
11. *Caroline's Scrapbook*, Vol. 15.
12. *New York Times*, March 13, 1874.
13. Severance, *Millard Fillmore Papers*, Vol. XI, p. 476.

FURTHER READING

Casey, Jane Clark. *Millard Fillmore: Thirteenth President of the United States.* New York: Children's Press, 1988.

Deem, James M. *Millard Fillmore.* Berkeley Heights, New Jersey: Enslow Publishers, 2003.

Cleveland, Will and Mark Alvarez. *Yo, Millard Fillmore (And All Those Other Presidents You Don't Know).* Brookfield, Connecticut: Millbrook, 1997.

Joseph, Paul. *Millard Fillmore* (United States Presidents). Edina, Minnesota: Checkerboard Library, 2000.

Souter, Gerry and Janet. *Millard Fillmore: Our Thirteenth President.* Chanhassen, Minnesota: Child's World, 2002.

INTERNET ADDRESSES

Internet Public Library article on Millard Fillmore
<http://www.ipl.org/div/potus/mfillmore.html>

Online biography of Abigail Powers Fillmore
<http://www.firstladies.org/Bibliography/AbigailFillmore/FLMain.htm>

American Presidents' biography of Millard Fillmore
<http://www.americanpresidents.org/presidents/president.asp?PresidentNumber=13>

Official White House biography of Millard Fillmore
<http://www.whitehouse.gov/history/presidents/mf13.html>

<http://ap.grolier.com/presidents/ea/bios/13fillm.html>

<http://www.millardfillmorehouse.org.>

PLACES TO VISIT

NEW YORK

Millard Fillmore Honeymoon Cottage, East Aurora. Located on Shearer Avenue, this is the only remaining home of the Fillmores, other than the White House. It is also the only presidential home made by the president himself. You can see the split lath construction in a peek-a-boo window into the wall. In the library is one of the mahogany bookcases and a couch from Abigail's White House Library, as well as the rosewood square piano and Abby's harp and music stand, gifts from Hiram. Open Wednesday, Saturday, and Sunday 2 P.M. to 4 P.M., June through October. (716) 652-8875.

Buffalo and Erie County Historical Society, Buffalo. Located at 25 Nottingham Court, this historical society owes its beginnings to Fillmore and holds many remembrances of him in the museum. Upstairs look for him in a mural with Lincoln. You can get a sense of Fillmore's early life from the pioneer display. The "Street of 1870" display includes a full-size model of Millard Fillmore by his black coupe. There are also many fascinating details about the Underground Railroad in the "Neighbors" exhibit, including a map showing a major route going right through East Aurora to Buffalo. A display about the Know Nothing Party lets you use their secret code to decode secret questions. (716) 873-9644.

Michigan Avenue Baptist Church, Buffalo. This church, located at 511 Michigan Avenue, is a confirmed spot on the Underground Railroad, which was active during Fillmore's lifetime. From here you can walk to Broderick Park at the foot of Ferry Street, and see the Niagara River, where "conductors" on the Underground Railroad helped escaped slaves cross to freedom.

Forest Lawn Cemetery, Buffalo. The Fillmore grave is located in the beautiful Forest Lawn Cemetery at Delaware Park in Buffalo. Look in Section F for a pink granite obelisk surrounded by an iron fence. It centers and divides two rows of graves—Abigail, her mother, Abby, and Powers on the west; and Millard and Caroline on the east. (716) 885-1600.

Genesee Country Museum, Mumford. Visit the Pioneer's Cabin to see the primitive life of New York's early settlers. The Red Schoolhouse is similar to the schoolhouse where Fillmore taught. Also Millard's law office looked much like the Delancy Stow Law & Insurance Office, circa 1825. (585) 538-6822. <http://www.geneseecountryvillage.org>.

Lockport Locks & Canal Tours, Lockport. This canal boat tour business is located on Market Street. Spend two summer hours riding the Erie Canal, which was constructed during Fillmore's lifetime. You will hear fascinating details about the history and science of the locks, and the process of going through the double locks is amazing—high technology for one hundred eighty years ago. (716) 433-6155.

Fillmore Glen State Park, Moravia. Located on Route 38, this state park is named for Millard Fillmore, who was born in a cabin five miles to the east. There is a replica of the Fillmore family cabin on the park grounds. (315) 497-0130.

Schuyler Mansion, Albany. Located at 32 Catherine Street, this historic home is where Fillmore's wedding to Caroline McIntosh took place. Alexander Hamilton also married Betsy Schuyler here. (518) 434-0834.

INDEX